W. F. Crafts

The Bible and the Sunday school

W. F. Crafts

The Bible and the Sunday school

ISBN/EAN: 9783337171810

Printed in Europe, USA, Canada, Australia, Japan

Cover: Foto ©Lupo / pixelio.de

More available books at **www.hansebooks.com**

THE BIBLE

AND

THE SUNDAY SCHOOL.

BY

Rev. Richard Newton, D.D.
Rev. Lyman Abbott, D.D.
James Hughes, Esq.
Rev. F. A. O'Meara, D.D.
P. P. Bliss.
Miss Frances E. Willard.
Rev. A. H. Munro.
Rev. J. L. Hurlbut.
J. E. Searles, Jr.

Rev. Henry Ward Beecher.
M. C. Hazard, Esq.
Rev. Jno. H. Castle, D.D.
Rev. J. E. Latimer, D.D.
A. O. VanLennep, Esq.
Rev. H. M. Parsons, D.D.
Rev. F. H. Marling.
Miss M. E. Winslow.
Rev. E. O. Haven, D.D.
Rev. C. H. Payne, D.D.

Rev. W. F. Crafts.
Rev. S. L. Gracey.
Mrs. W. F. Crafts.
Rev. B. P. Raymond.
Miss Jenny B. Merrill.
C. M. Morton, Esq.
Rev. H. W. Warren, D.D.
Rev. D. Marvin, Jr.
Hon. A. D. Shaw.

EDITED BY

REV. W. F. CRAFTS.

Gather the people together, men and women, and children, and thy stranger that *is* within thy gates, that they may hear, and that they may learn, and fear the LORD your God, and observe to do all the words of this law : and *that* their children, which have not known *any thing*, may hear, and learn to fear the LORD your God, as long as ye live in the land whither ye go over Jordan to possess it.—DEUT. xxxi, 12, 13.

LEE & SHEPARD, Publishers,

41-45 Franklin Street, Boston.   678 Broadway, New York.

SECOND EDITION.

HUNTER, ROSE & CO.,
PRINTERS,
25 WELLINGTON STREET WEST,
TORONTO.

PREFACE.

The lecture outlines in this little volume are epitomes of addresses and conversations given at the Sunday School Parliament, Rev. W. F. Crafts, Conductor, held July 18–26, 1876, on Wellesley Island, one of the famous "Thousand Islands," in the St. Lawrence River.

It is thought that in the present form of "Outlines," the "points made" will be more permanently and widely useful as a basis for study in teachers' meetings, normal classes, and institutes, as well as for private reading, than in the usual form of a consecutive and detailed "report."

Parents, Pastors, Bible Students and Sunday School workers will find in these outlines many valuable hints and suggestions, which may be further developed by thought and experience. Methods of Bible study will be found to have equal prominence with methods of Sunday School work.

CONTENTS.

I.—THE BIBLE, THE WORD OF GOD.   PAGE.
   1. Science confirming the Scriptures 1
   2. The Bible's Divine Character shown in its history   6

II.—THE BIBLE AND ITS STUDENTS.
   1. Structure and arrangement of the Bible.......... 7
   2. Manners and Customs of Bible times 12
   3. Geography of the Bible........................ 12
   4. Revision of the Bible......................... 13
   5. Principles of Interpretation 15
   6. Reasons for Bible Reading. Methods of Bible Reading. Comprehensive Bible Reading.......... 17
   7. Topical Bible Reading........................ 24
   8. Bagster's Scripture Index 26
   9. "Bible Readings" in their various uses........ 32
  10. Bible Marking............................... 41
  11. Personal Study of the Lesson 44
  12. Adults as Bible Students in the Sunday School.... 45
  13. Further Hints on How to Study the Bible........ 47
  14. Bill of Fare from the Bible................... 48

III.—THE BIBLE AND ITS TEACHERS.
   1. Hints on the Public use of the Bible............. 52
   2. The Pastor's Relation to the Sunday School 53

III.—THE BIBLE AND ITS TEACHERS (*continued*).

		PAGE.
3.	Using the Bible with Enquirers	54
4.	"How can we get rid of Incompetent Teachers?"	56
5.	Three Requisites in Religious Teaching	57
6.	Conditions of Teaching with power	58
7.	Normal Class Training for Teachers	61
8.	Qualities and Training of Primary Teachers	62
9.	Attention, Discipline, and Questioning	63
10.	Illustrative Teaching	64
11.	Importance and Method of Public Reviews	67
12.	What the Sunday School Teacher may learn from Secular Schools	70
13.	A Study of Christ as the Model Teacher	86
14.	Spiritual Work in the Sunday School	89
15.	The Sunday School Teacher's Decalogue	90
16.	Chart for Preachers and Teachers	91

IV.—THE BIBLE AND CHILDHOOD.

1.	The Bible Estimate of Childhood	92
2.	"How shall we Manage Unruly Boys in the Sunday Schools?"	97
3.	"How can we get Pupils to Study their Lessons at Home?"	97
4.	"How can a more general attendance of Children at preaching be secured?"	100
5.	Preaching to Children	102
6.	The Lesson of the Primary Class	103
7.	Conversion of Children	107
8.	Culture of Converted Children	109
9.	Home Christian Culture	112
10.	The Sunday School and the Home	114

V.—THE BIBLE AND SUNDAY SCHOOL MACHINERY.

1. The Name of the Sunday School 120
2. Sunday School Rooms and Library Plan 121
3. Constitution 121
4. Programme 122
5. Financial System and Culture of Benevolence 123
6. Music for General School and for Primary Class.... 125
7. Sunday School Concerts 126
8. Printing Press Helps in Sunday School Work 127
9. Organization of Primary Class 134
10. The Value and use of Sociables 135
11. An Ancient Religious Convention 135

VI.—THE BIBLE AND THE WORLD.

1. The Bible and the Public Schools 147
2. Christian Temperance Work 150
3. The Bible and Universal Brotherhood 151

APPENDIX.

Thousand Island Park and the Sunday School Parliament 158

The Bible and the Sunday School.

EDITED BY

REV. W. F. CRAFTS.

OPINIONS OF THE PRESS.

Thus collected and arranged they are likely to prove useful to all who have anything to do with Sunday Schools.—*Globe.*

Every pastor and teacher should have this book. It contains a thousand useful hints.—*London Advertiser.*

Parents, pastors, Bible students, and Sunday School workers will find in these outlines many valuable hints and suggestions, which may be further developed by thought and experience for the benefit of all.—*Jamestown Daily Journal.*

Every pastor, superintendent, teacher, and every Christian who would read his Bible to best advantage, should order the book.—*Guelph Weekly Mercury.*

It contains the points made at that Parliament by the able and eloquent speakers, and is calculated to be eminently useful to Sunday School teachers and conductors of normal classes. Parents, pastors, Bible students, and all Sunday School workers will find it a great help. We commend it to these and the general public.—*Brantford Weekly Expositor.*

It should prove particularly interesting to those engaged in Sunday School work.—*Daily News* (Kingston).

It is specially designed as a basis of study for teachers' meetings, etc. The book will be a highly valuable one to teachers and others interested in Sunday School work.—*Hamilton Spectator.*

A really wonderful little work of one hundred and seventy pages, edited by Rev. W. F. Crafts, a clergyman well known throughout the country for his interest in Sunday Schools. The work suggests not only thought, but methods. It is intended to systematize much work that is now poorly done, because of the crude ideas prevailing as to how it ought to be done. In this respect alone, every teacher of a class in the Sabbath School will find this little work of valuable assistance to him.—*St. John's Globe* (*N.B.*).

It will be of great service to Sunday School workers.—*Christian Home Journal* (Philadelphia).

Among the names of those whose utterances at the Parliament are here published, we observe that of Henry Ward Beecher, of Lyman Abbott, and James Hughes, Esq. (Inspector of Public Schools in Toronto). We heartily commend it to the attention of our readers.—*Religious Herald* (Hartford).

There is a great deal of very choice matter in it. Indeed, we do not know where so much of condensed thought, facts, principles, hints and suggestions in relation to the Bible, its character, value, method of study, and way to use it, can be found as in this. It is indeed *multum in parvo.*—*The Standard, Chicago.*

LECTURE OUTLINES

ON

The Bible and the Sunday School.

I. THE BIBLE, THE WORD OF GOD.

Its Inspiration. 2 Timothy iii. 16, 17 ; 2 Peter i. 20, 21 ; Romans xv. 4 ; 1 Cor. x. 11 ; Ephesians vi. 17 ; 1 Thes. ii. 13.

Its Sufficiency. Luke xvi. 31 ; Deut. iv. 2 ; Prov. xxx. 5, 6 ; Rev. xxii. 17–19.

Its Power. John xv. 3 ; xvii. 17 ; Eph. v. 26 ; Jer. xxiii. 29 ; Heb. iv. 12 ; Psalm xix. 7–11.

Our Need of It. Psalm cxix. 18 ; Luke xxiv. 45 ; John vi. 63 ; 2 Cor. iii. 5, 6.

Its Use, and Our Duty towards It. Nehem. viii. 8, and ix. 2, 3 ; 2 Chron. xvii. 9 ; 1 Peter iv. 11 ; Acts. xviii. 28, and xvii. 11, 12 : 2 Cor. ii. 17 ; Deut. vi. 6, 7, and xxix. 29 ; Joshua i. 8 ; Psalm i. 2 ; 1 Peter ii. 1, 2 ; Col. iii. 16 ; Psalm cxix. 1, 2, 9, 11, etc.

1. SCIENCE CONFIRMING THE SCRIPTURES.

BY REV. H. W. WARREN, D.D.

Years of discussion have established these two principles :

(I.) The Bible no where opposes demonstrated Science.

(II.) The Bible always has been, and is yet, far in advance of the attainments of Science, even in advance of man's ability to understand its plain declarations.

These are remarkable propositions. If they are maintained there is no more ground for contention. There must be wisdom from God in its pages.

The Bible was written in ages of ignorance of the sciences of to-day, by unlearned men, in a great part, and it would be simply impossible for them, as men, to avoid statements in opposition to the knowledge and discoveries of to-day. Even wise men could not do it. Pythagoras, and the wise men of his day, taught that the earth was flat. And the wise men of our day have taught within the remembrance of many of us, that marine shells, found in the high mountains, were proof of the Noahcian deluge. Voltaire showed his fitness to lead a scientific assault on the Bible, by declaring that these shells were brought to their places in the mountains, by the crowds of pilgrims from the Holy Land! Indeed, there is hardly an established truth in science to-day, concerning which men have not uttered many erroneous opinions. I do not affirm that the Bible does not speak of some things according to visual appearance, as the sunrise and sunset. But our nautical almanacs and other scientific treatises do the same thing to-day. I do not deny that some interpretations, and even translations of the Scripture, have been contradictory to demonstrated science. For how can we truly translate from a foreign language, things we could not understand, if written plainly in our own? It needs knowledge to read scientific statements. But, uniformly, that translation which has harmonized with science has been found to be the truer one. Indeed, the translations of many scriptural texts have been very difficult, because we lacked the knowledge to make their real signification seem possible to our thought. Discovering the scientific truth, we returned to the Scripture, and its meaning was clear as sunlight. Several passages which seemed, when fairly translated, to teach error, or to be poetical flights, have since been proved to be statements of literal facts. The Bible has been routed from many a position it never held, discovered to be impregnably intrenched, after its rout had been heralded. This will repeatedly appear in illustrating the second proposition. That the Bible could avoid error proclaims that God was in all its writing. How much more that it could always be in advance of science and discovery. Let us see if this second proposition is capable of proof. The Bible has asserted from the first, that creation of matter preceded arrangement. It was chaos, void, without form, darkness. Arrangement was a subsequent matter. The world was not created in the form it was to have. It was to be moulded, shaped, stratified, mountained, and vallied, subsequently. All of which science utters ages afterwards. The Bible has been sneered at a thousand years, for saying that light existed before the sun was outlined and limited. But now, men are praised for asserting the same thing. Peans are sung to La Place, that belong to God, and which are sung to God by angels, and all others who know that the Bible is older science than the *Mecanique Celeste*. It is a recently elucidated idea of science that the strata of the earth were formed by the action of water, and the mountains were once under the ocean. It is an idea long familiar to Bible readers. "Thou coverest the earth with the deep as with a garment. The waters stood above the mountains. At Thy rebuke they fled; at the voice of Thy thunder they hasted away. The mountains ascend, the valleys descend unto the place Thou hast founded for them." The whole volume of geology in a paragraph! Volumes of demonstrations of the impossibility of the Deluge might have been saved if men had been willing to read the explanations of God, by Peter: "For of this they are *willingly ignorant* that by the word of God there were heavens of old, and land framed out of water and by means of water, whereby *the world that then was*, being overflowed by water perished;"—a geological subsidence—"but the heavens that now are and the land"—the present geological upheaval—"by His word are kept for fire, &c." Every difficulty vanishes. It is a single sentence of geologic history, foretold and arranged by God for a specific time and purpose, and no more difficult than upheavals and subsidences that have occurred in our day. Ages on ages man's wisdom held the earth to be flat. Meanwhile God was saying, century after century, of Himself, "He sitteth upon the sphere of the earth." [Gesenius.] Men racked their feeble wits for expedients to uphold the earth, and the best they could devise were serpents, elephants, and turtles. Meanwhile God was perpetually telling men that he had "hung the earth upon nothing."

Men were ever trying to number the stars. Hipparcus counted 1022, Ptolemy 1026. And it is easy to number those visible to the naked eye. But the Bible said that they were, as the sands of the sea, "innumerable." Science has appliances of enumeration unknown to other ages, but the space penetrating telescopes reveal more worlds: eighteen millions in a single system, and systems beyond count, till men acknowledge that the stars are innumerable to man. It is God's prerogative "to number all the stars. He also calleth them all by their names."

Torricelli's discovery, that the air had weight, was received with incredulity. For ages the air had propelled ships, thrust itself against the bodies of men, and overturned their works. But no man ever dreamed that weight was necessary to give momentum. During all the centuries it had stood in the Bible, waiting for man's comprehension: "He gave to the air its weight." [Job xxviii. 25].

The pet science of to-day is meteorology. The fluctuations and variations of the weather have hitherto baffled all attempts at unravelling. It has seemed that there was no law in the fickle changes. But at length perseverance and skill have triumphed, and a single man in one place predicts the weather and winds for a continent. But the Bible has always insisted that the whole department was under law. Nay, it laid down that law so clearly, that if men had been willing to learn from it, they might have reached this wisdom ages ago. The whole moral law is not more clearly crystallized in, "Thou shalt love the Lord thy God with all thy heart, and thy neighbour as thyself," than all the fundamentals of the science of meteorology are crystallized in this word: "The wind goeth toward the south (equator), and turneth about (up) unto the north; it whirleth about continually; and the wind returneth again according to his circuits (established routes). All the rivers run into the sea, yet the sea is not full. Unto the place whence the rivers come, thither return they again." [Eccles. i. 6, 7.]

That the central part of the earth was molten fire was received with great hesitation; and even now, after numerous proofs, is by some minds hotly contested. But God knows, and he says, "Out of the earth cometh bread, but at the same time underneath, it turns itself as fire" [Job xxviii. 5]. Long before it was supposed that rock could be melted, the Bible declared that "the hills melted like wax." "Poetic figure," says the rhetorician. "Literal truth," says the laborious chemist.

That light makes music in its passage is asserted by God to Job, by science more than three thousand years afterwards. Poets Shakspeare, Byron, Milton, Addison, Mrs. Browning, Willis, and others, have uttered the conception as a fancy; the Bible and science as fact. The Word is a golconda of gems. Beautiful the thought and words of him who mines it.

"There's not the smallest orb that thou beholdest,
But in his motion like an angel sings."—A.D. 1596 (?)

"The morning stars sang together."—3000 years earlier.

God's statement that the sun's "going is from the end of the heaven, and his circuit on the ends of it," has given edge to many a sneer at its supposed assertion, that the sun went round the earth. It teaches a higher truth. Let pigmies learn the truth of alpine proportions, that the sun itself is but a superior planet, and flies in a path of eighteen millions of years, from one end of the heavens to the other, around the Pleiades as its sun. Confounded Job, a puny sick man, could answer nothing when asked if he could bind the sweet influences of the Pleiades. He did not know that they swung millions of suns and their attendant worlds.

When I hear so eminent an astronomer, and so true a Christian, as Mitchell, who understood the voices, in which the heavens declare the glory of God, as his own vernacular tongue, who read the significance of God's embodied word with delight, and who fed upon God's written word, as his daily bread; when I hear him declare, "we find an aptness and propriety in all these astronomical illustrations, which are not weakened but amazingly strengthened, when viewed in the full light of our present knowledge;" when I hear Herschel declare, "all human discoveries seem to be made only for the purpose of confirming more strongly the truths that come from on high, and are contained in the sacred writings," I ask, who is he that declares that the Bible and science are at variance? I shall probably find that he is ignorant of both. God has scattered brief notes of His works in the Bible. Man's discoveries are but illustration and comment.

"The city was pure gold like unto clear glass." [Rev. xxi. 18.] How many sneers the Bible has endured for such a statement! It could bide its time. Truths always can. Faraday has demonstrated that fine gold may become perfectly transparent like clear glass. And some of the most beautiful productions in ruby glass are produced by solutions of gold.

Whatever point we touch sheds confirmation on the Book that gives a light to every age. "It gives, but borrows none." It must be the wisdom of Omniscience behind it; the Mind that knows the end from the beginning.

2. THE BIBLE'S DIVINE CHARACTER SHOWN IN ITS HISTORY.*

This subject is so full of incidents that a fair treatment of the question would require the space of this whole volume. A most interesting personal study or public lecture may be prepared by hiring or buying the fifteen large diagrams and pictures on "The Literary History of the Bible," of the London or American Sunday School Union, at some of their depositaries; buying also or hiring the following books:—"The Book and Its Story," "Leaves from the Book and Its Story," "Our English Bible," "Bible in many Tongues," and "Farmer Tomkins and his Bibles."

II. THE BIBLE AND ITS STUDENTS.

SEARCH THE SCRIPTURES, John 5: 39. John 2: 12, 13.
EARNESTLY, Josh. 1: 8. Psa. 119: 12.
ANXIOUSLY, John 20: 31. Psa. 119: 9.
REGULARLY, Acts 17: 11. Psa. 1: 2.
CAREFULLY, Luke 24: 27. 2 Tim. 3: 16, 17.
HUMBLY, Luke 24: 45. James 1: 22.

---

* This subject was ably presented at the Parliament by Rev. S. L. Gracey.

Structure and Arrangement of the Bible.

A Normal Class Paper, by Rev. J. H. Vincent, D.D.*

(I.) The Sacred Canon.

(1.) There are **many possible methods** by which an all wise Creator might communicate to man a knowledge of His character and will.

(2.) The way in which our Creator has seen fit to reveal Himself to man is by **a supernatural history** produced on the earth under His immediate direction, and then under the same divine direction and inspiration recorded in a series of books.

(3.) This history, thus recorded, having a religious aim, will of necessity contain **a great variety**, as to its subject-matter. It will have history, geography, biography, doctrine, ethics, poetry, prophecy, etc.

(4.) The human mind produces many books, containing human deductions, speculations, imaginations, etc., etc. Some claim to be the results of reason; others to be the revelations of God, or of the gods; while some of them are the productions of minds intent upon deception and mischief, whatever they may profess.

(5.) If, therefore, the true God should give a true book for human instruction there **must be evidences that it is truly from God**, so that men may distinguish between it and the false or defective works of man. There must be a rule or standard by which we may certainly know just what books are human and what are divine.

(6.) Therefore we have what is called the Canon of Scripture.
    (*a.*) The word **"Canon"** signifies literally **a straight line**, a rule, a law, a standard.

---

* Those who contemplate organizing a Normal Class should write to Rev. J. H. Vincent, D.D., 805 Broadway, N.Y., for a catalogue of his Normal Class papers and books, which form the completest system of training for religious teachers ever prepared. This paper was presented and taught at the Parliament by the Rev. J. L. Hurlbut, of Plainfield, N.J.

(*b.*) The Scripture itself is **a canon or rule of life**, the authoritative standard of religion and morality.

(*c.*) The **tests**, rules, or standards by which we determine that it is in whole or in part from God are called the " Canon of Scripture."

(*d.*) The several books which are thus examined and proved to be genuine and authentic are called " The Sacred Canon."

There are many

(II.) EVIDENCES WHICH SUSTAIN THE CLAIM OF THE BIBLE BELIEVER

That the book on which he rests is from God. (1.) It has **long** been **accepted** as divine by the Church—both Jewish and Christian. (2.) It has **stood** the most **searching tests** of friends and foes for centuries. (3.) Exposed by various translations and by sectarian interests to the liability of interpolation and change it **remains** essentially **the same**. Its "various readings" do not affect the great doctrines which it contains. (4.) Its **internal character**, unity, purity, marvellous moral standards, fidelity to human nature, etc., etc., prove its divinity. (5.) **Its adaptation to human needs** and its effects upon the race wherever permitted to exert its energies, abundantly demonstrate that it is not a human production. (6.) It is in striking **harmony with true science**. The facts of nature, and of human nature, and of human history, sustain the claims of the book. (7.) To the **personal experience** of all who have tested and trusted it we may safely appeal. The Bible is the missing keystone in individual and in social life. Once inserted, it proves that He who made man and put him into this world, also made the Bible as his safeguard and stay.

There are ten

(III.) NAMES BY WHICH THE BOOK OF GOD IS KNOWN.

These are divided into four classes.

(1.) From the **material** used in making ancient books it is called the Bible.

"*Bible*"—is from the Greek word *biblos*, a book. "The name was given originally, like *liber* in Latin, to the inner bark of the linden or teil tree, and afterwards to the bark of the papyrus, the materials of which early books were sometimes made." Chrysostom, in the fourth or fifth century, first applied the term "Biblia" to the whole collection of sacred books.

(2.) From the **mode of revealing and recording** the Revelation it is called the Oracles and the Scriptures.

"*Oracle*"—from the Latin word *oro*, to speak: *os, oris*, the mouth. The sanctuary of the tabernacle and the temple was called the *oracle*. 1 Kings vi. 16; Psalm xxviii. 2. The term is used in the New Testament to designate the revelations of God. Acts vii. 38; 1 Peter iv. 11. For the heathen use of the word, see "*oracle*" in any dictionary or encyclopædia.

"*Scriptures*,"—Latin, *scribo*, I write—*Scriptus*. The Jews called their sacred books *Kethib*, written, or *mikra*, gathering.

(3.) From the **contents** of the Book it is called the Word, the Law, Prophets, and Psalms, and the Testaments or Covenants.

"*Testament.*"—The word *diatheke*, which we now translate *testament*, signifies either a testament or a covenant. Covenant—an agreement, a mutual arrangement; two Testaments, old and new. "Not two distinct and unrelated covenants, but merely the *former* and the *latter* dispensations of the one grand covenant of mercy."—*Bush*.

(4.) From the **character** of the book it is called the *Bible*, the Holy Bible, and the Canonical Scriptures.

(IV.) There are three

CLASSIFICATIONS OF THE BOOKS OF THE BIBLE.

(1.) **In the Bible itself.** See 2 Cor. iii. 14; 2 Cor. iii. 6; Zech. vii. 12; Matt. xi. 13; Matt. xxii. 40; Acts xiii. 15; Luke xxiv. 44.

(2.) The **recognised Jewish classification.**
    (1.) The Law :—The five books of Moses.
    (2.) The Prophets :—
        (1.) The *former* Prophets :—Joshua, Judges, Samuel, and Kings.
        (2.) The *latter* Prophets :—Greater and Minor.
    (3.) Hagiographa :—
        (1.) First class :—Psal., Prov., and Job.
        (2.) Second class :—Sol. Song, Ruth, Lam., Eccl., and Es.
        (3.) Third class :—Dan., Ez., Neh., and Chron.

(3.) **The order of our version.**
    (1.) The Old Testament :—
        (1.) The Pentateuch—G. E. L. N. D.—5.
        (2.) The Historical—J. J. R. S. K. C. E. N. E.—12.
        (3.) The Poetical—J. P. P. E. S.—5.
        (4.) The Prophetical—1. Greater :—I. J. (L.) E. D.—5. 2. Minor :—H. J. A. O. J. M. N. H. Z. H. Z. M.—12.
    (2.) The New Testament :—
        (1.) The Historical—M. M. L. J. A.—5.
        (2.) The Pauline Epistles—R. C. G. E. P. C. T. T. T. P. H.—14.
        (3.) The General or Catholic Epistles—J. P. J. J.—7.
        (4.) The Prophetical—R.—1.

(V.) THE CONTENTS OF THE BIBLE.

(1.) **God the Creator and Father is revealed** in the Old Testament as ruler of men and nations, preparing the world for the advent of the Son.

(2.) **God the Son is revealed** in the four "Gospels" of the New Testament as Prophet, Priest, and King of men, living, dying, rising from the dead, ascending into the heavens, promising before his departure to send the Holy Ghost to abide with his faithful followers on the earth.

(3.) **God the Holy Ghost is revealed** in the "Acts" and in the "Epistles" of the New Testament as inspirer and comforter and almighty protector of the Church in the earth.

(4.) **God the Father, Son, and Holy Ghost—the one God—is revealed** in the last book of the Bible—"The Revelation"—as governing and directing all things of earth and heaven in the interest of the people of God, who, redeemed from sin, shall reign for ever in spotless purity, unbroken fellowship, unalloyed blessedness, for ever doing and delighting in the will of God.

BLACKBOARD EPITOME OF THE ABOVE PAPER.

(As it would stand after it had been developed by a drill of the Class.)

(I.) CANON OF SCRIPTURE.

(a.) Meaning, line, rule, law.
(b.) Scripture is canon of life.
(c.) Tests.
(d.) The name applied.

(II.) THE EVIDENCES.

(1.) L. A.; (2) S. S. T.; (3) R. S.; (4) I. C.; (5) A. H. N.; (6.) H. T. S.; (7) P. E.

(III.) NAMES.

B. O. S. T. W. ; T. L. ; L. P. P. ; T. C. ; T. B. ; H. B. ; C. S.

(IV.) CLASSIFICATION.

(1.) B.
(2.) J.—L. 5 B. M ; P. F. J. J. S. K. ; L. G., M. H. 1. Psa., P. J. ; 2. Sol. S. R. L. Ec. Es. ; 3. D. Ez. N. Ch.
(3.) Order of our version—O. T., N. T.

(V.) CONTENTS.

(1.) God Rev. in O. T. as ruler.
(2.) God S. in Gospels as P. P. K.
(3.) God H. G. in Acts as Insp. C. P.
(4.) God F. S. H. G. in Rev.

2. MANNERS AND CUSTOMS OF BIBLE TIMES.

As this subject requires too many illustrations to be treated even briefly in these pages, we can only indicate the helps to its study.

1. Illustrated Lectures on Oriental Customs, Costumes, Manners, Implements, &c. By A. O. Van Lennep, Montclair, N. J., a native of Syria ; or by Rev. J. S. Ostrander, Haarlem, N. Y., both of whom lecture at very reasonable prices.

2. Dr. Van Lennep's great work, published by Harper Brothers, New York ; sold also by Adam Miller & Co., Toronto.

3. Cheaper books on this subject are : "Freeman's Handbook of Bible Customs," Nelson & Phillips, N. Y. ; or "Thomson's Land and Book (2 vols.), Harper Brothers, N. Y. ; also for sale by Adam Miller & Co., Toronto.

3. BIBLE GEOGRAPHY.

Whitney's "Handbook of Bible Geography," Nelson & Phillips, N. Y., is an inexpensive and excellent treatment of this whole subject.

4. REVISION OF THE BIBLE.*

BY REV. F. A. O'MEARA, D.D.

(1.) There is a very strong **repugnance** among Christians against any interference with the authorized version of our Bible. But, notwithstanding this, it is desirable that our version should be brought as near to the meaning and spirit of the original as the present state of Biblical scholarship will admit. This is required by loyalty to the text as it came from the hand of the inspired writers.

---

* This vastly important task had its origin in the Convocation of Canterbury of the Church of England, in 1870. The late Dean Alford, Archbishop Trench, Bishop Ellicott, Professors Lightfoot, Hort, Kennedy, and others, were appointed by the Convocation a committee, with power to associate other scholars from various denominations with them, for the purpose of revising the translation of the Scriptures now in common use, and known as King James' Version. In 1871 Dr. Phillip Schaff was requested to form an American Committee, to co-operate with the English Committee in this task. He did so, and divided the American Committee into two Companies—one to work on the Old Testament and the other to work on the New Testament. Both Companies meet during most of the year monthly, in the Bible House, in this city, and prosecute their labours during two or three days. In the summer, however, they avoid the heat and noise of the great metropolis by holding a session of a week in length in some town where one of their members resides, and to which he invites them. Thus the Old Testament Company met in '73 at New Haven, in '74 at Princeton, in '75 at Andover, and last week at New Brunswick.

The character of this Company is thoroughly unsectarian and Catholic. It embraces the most distinguished scholars and representative men of the great denominations, and, therefore, is eminently fitted to aid in completing a broad and comprehensive work. The Chairman of the Old Testament Company is Professor Green, of Princeton, and the other members are as follows, being named in alphabetical order : Dr. Aiken, of the Theological Seminary at Princeton ; Dr. Chambers, one of the pastors of the Collegiate Church, New York ; Dr. Conant, of Philadelphia ; Dr. Day, of the Theological Seminary at New Haven ; Dr. De Witt, of the Theological Seminary at New Brunswick ; Dr. Hare, of Philadelphia ; Dr. Krauth, of the University of Pennsylvania ; Dr. Lewis, of Union College at Schenectady ; Dr. Mead, of the Theological Seminary at Andover ; Dr. Packard, of the Theological Seminary, Alexandria, Va., ; Dr. Osgood, of the University at Rochester ; Dr. Strong, of the Drew Theological Seminary, and Dr. Van Dyke, a missionary and learned Oriental scholar in Syria.

Not all of these gentlemen are or can be equally regular in attending the meetings. Thus Dr. Conant and Dr. Taylor Lewis (the latter on account of his health) are seldom present, and Dr. Van Dyke is obliged, of course, to make his suggestions by letter.

The method of doing the work is exceedingly thorough, and will, therefore, no doubt, prove generally satisfactory. The British Committee sends printed copies of their revision to the American Committee, who go over it with the greatest care and conscientiousness, making such suggestions of alteration and improvement as they deem advisable. A bare majority of the Committee is enough in the first instance to establish a tentative or provisional reading. At some subsequent meeting, however, after the members have had renewed opportunity to re-examine the passage, the provisional reading is taken up again, fully and deliberately considered, and then adopted or rejected by a *two-thirds* majority. The work is then transmitted back to England for final examination and decision by the English Committee. If there still remain a few exceptional difficulties, they are made the subject of correspondence and thus of final agreement.

The work of the American scholars is said to be very satisfactory to their English

(2.) The task assigned is **not really a revision of the Bible**, which is the work of God, and cannot be either revised or improved. Nor is it really the production of a new translation, since the authorized version is very nearly perfect. The purpose in this movement is rather to perfect the authorized version in those few points where a fuller knowledge of the original language, or a change in the use of English words, makes a change necessary. In this connection let it be remembered that our present translation is the production of many revisions.

(3.) Our present version requires revision in the following respects:—

(*a*) **Passages are to be omitted that are not found in the oldest and best manuscripts.** It should be said here that these omissions will not weaken a single Christian doctrine. 1 John v. 7 should be erased for this reason.

(*b*) **Some passages require change to bring them into accord with the most ancient MSS.** For example—Rev. xxii. 14, should be not "blessed are they that *do* his commandments," which sounds like salvation by works, but rather "blessed are they that have washed their robes," as in the earliest manuscripts.

(*c*) **Some original words have been incorrectly translated.** For example—1 Thess. v. 22, should be "abstain from every form of evil." Most of these changes are those of tenses and cases which do not affect the doctrine presented in the least.

---

brethren. Nearly all the suggestions made by the former have been adopted by the latter. The entire work is carried on in a reverent and conservative spirit, only those changes being decided upon which are deemed absolutely necessary, and which give a clearer and more accurate equivalent in English of the original Hebrew and Greek. Of the two Committees the British is the more conservative in clinging to old words and usages; while the American is more radical, or, at least, more in sympathy with the changes in words and idioms about to be made in the near future. The Old Testament Company spent four days in the Sage Library, at New Brunswick, in severe labour from 9 A.M. until 5 P.M. each day, and concluded their work by finishing the revision of the 100th Psalm. They have now, therefore, gone through the Pentateuch and one hundred of the Psalms. The New Testament Company have thus far revised the Gospels, the Acts, the Epistle to the Romans, and the Pastoral Epistles.

It is not possible for us to give the changes or different readings, inasmuch as details of this kind are kept secret, very properly, until the final work shall be given to the public. The entire work will probably require five years yet for its completion; though it is quite likely that the Psalms or the Pentateuch, or both, will at no distant date be published as specimens of the great task in hand.

(*d*) Some passages, which very correctly and intelligibly represented the meaning of the original two and a half centuries ago, have, through the **changes in the English language,** ceased to do so to the modern reader, and therefore need revision. For example—" they took up their *carriages*" for "they packed their baggage," and "he that letteth will let," for "he that hindereth will hinder."

This centennial period of the Republic will be marked by the production of the authorized version of future generations, which will have been the production of English and American learned men and divines working in unison in London and New York, furnishing another bond of union between the two countries.

5. Principles of Bible Interpretation.

BY REV. LYMAN ABBOTT, D.D.[*]

Looking at the Bible from the human side, we should remember that it was

Written,
Copied,
Translated,
Printed
} by man.

Hence the following points should be observed in its interpretation:—

(1.) Have **a well-printed Bible.** "The Teachers' Bible" of the American Tract Society and "Bagster's Bible" are the best.

(2.) Get at **the best translation.** *a.* By studying it in "the original," if possible. *b.* By comparing the received translations with the new translations that are appearing. *c.* By comparison also with French and German Bibles, especially "Luther's Bible." *d.* By examining modern commentaries, through which those who are without scholastic training can get at the true rendering.

---

[*] Author of "Illustrated Commentary on Acts," also "Commentary on Matthew and Mark," "Jesus of Nazareth," "Dictionary of Religious Knowledge," &c.

(3.) Ascertain if you have a **correct copy**.

There are from 120,000 to 800,000 variations in the various copies of the Bible, mostly unimportant typographical errors, and not one of them affecting any Bible doctrine. 1 John v. 7, is now universally allowed to be an interpolation. These errors may be discovered by referring (a) to Tischendorf's Greek Testament, and (b) some critical commentary.

(4.) Study the **peculiar circumstances** of the writer of any passage under consideration.

(a) Ask "**Who is it that speaks in this passage?**" A Universalist preacher took as a text to preach against future punishment, Gen. iii. 4,—"Thou shalt not surely die"—the words of the devil. A judge once said in a charge to the jury, "We have the highest authority for saying "skin for skin, yea all that a man hath will he give for his life." The papers next day called attention to the fact that these words were uttered by the devil, adding—"Now we know who the judge regards as the highest authority."

(b) *Ask what is* **the character of the passage?** Law? Poetry? History? Philosophy? Why not interpret the poem in Judges v. 20, by the same prose laws that so many apply to the poem in Josh. x. 13?

(c) Ask "What is **the temperament of the writer or speaker?**" Rom. ix. 3 is to be read in the light of Paul's vehement nature, not used as a prose statement of a necessary principle of didactic theology. So John vi. 53, 63 is to be read with Christ's illustrative temperament in mind.

(d) **The general aim** of the writer should also be kept in view.

(e) We must **put ourselves in the place of the original hearers or readers**, remembering their customs and prejudices. In reading the twenty-third Psalm, if we have before our minds New England sheep unprotected, unguarded, and given the roughest of pastures, instead of the Oriental flock and fold, we shall have anything but pleasant views of God as our Shepherd.

(f) **Compare Scripture with Scripture**, to find the

real Bible meaning of words and phrases. See Jas. i. 27, and Matt. xxiii. 23; Rom. xiii. 9, and Matt. xxii. 37–40. John xiv. 28, and John x. 30.

(*g*) **Take the plain and simple meaning** of a passage. Ingenious interpretations are usually dangerous.

(*h*) **Allow for yourself**, your prejudices, &c. The Calvinist reads Philippians ii. 12, 13, with all the emphasis on verse 13, while the Arminian accents verse 12, and reads verse 13 very lightly.

Apply these principles to Matt. xvi. 19.

	Spoken by	Therefore.
1.	Christ	Authoritative.
2.	Temperament,	Poetic.
3.	General aim,	Enfranchisement of **man**.
4.	Comparing Scripture,	"Keys"=power.
		"Kingdom"=allegiance.
		"Bind and loose"=forbidden and permitted.

Meaning :—

"I will give the power (keys) in thy life of allegiance to God (Kingdom of God), so that what you forbid yourself shall be forbidden, (bind) and what you permit yourself shall be permitted (loosed)." Compare Rom. viii. 1.

Looking at the Bible from the Divine side, we add two further principles of interpretation.

(*a*) **The object of the Bible** (2 Tim. iii. 16) prompts the question in our interpretation, "What spiritual effect am I to get or give from this passage?"

(*b*) **The author of the Bible**, being God, establishes the principle that its utterances are to be viewed as absolute truth.

6. Reasons and Methods for Bible Reading.

BY REV. W. F. CRAFTS.

Reasons :—

(1.) **For rock foundations of Christian experience.** "It is written," not "I feel," should be the basis of our hope and faith. Feelings change, but "The Word of God abideth for ever."

(2.) **To enrich our Christian testimony.** The Psalmist fitly calls the Scriptures "testimonies." Every experience of Christian life may be concisely and beautifully uttered in Scripture language. If a person commits to memory one new verse each day, beginning at three years of age, at seventy he will have learned 25,000 verses, that is, all the verses in the Bible suitable for memorising, there being 31,173 verses in all. Many families have begun this "verse-a-day" system, by repeating one verse a piece at the breakfast table each morning. The little volumes of "Daily Food," "Dew Drops" and others, with a verse for each day are helpful in this plan, each person having a different book each year, and each member of the family a different one at the same time.

(3.) **To enable us to help enquirers** with appropriate Scripture.*

(4.) **To provide ourselves with fitting words for the sick room.**

(5.) **To protect ourselves against temptation.** Luke iv. 1–13.

(6.) **To guard ourselves against the false standards** of character in modern literature.

METHODS :—

Notwithstanding all the reasons for Bible reading that have been mentioned, it is to many Christians a matter of duty rather than delight. What can we do to answer the prayer of Psalm cxix. 125, "Give me *relish* (literal) that I may know thy testimonies?" How can the experience of Psalm cxix. 24 be attained?

(1.) **Every one should have a reference Bible of his own,** strong enough to last a lifetime, and gather about it life-long associations.

(2.) **Every one should read the Bible with a purpose.**

---

* See article on "Use of Bible with Enquirers."

(3.) Read **the Bible through in course**, once or twice in a life-time, using 2 Tim. iii. 16, 17 as a personal glass through which to read each passage, asking "What reproof in this for me?" "What instruction?" &c.

(4.) Read **special portions of Scripture analytically**, looking into the deeper meanings, as astronomers search into the depths of the skies. New stars may be found in the most studied chapters.

(5.) Read the Bible with a view to **associate it with the scenes and surroundings** of our lives. Looking out upon Nature ask "What does the Bible say of trees and shrubs?" "What does the Bible say of rivers and waters?" So of national affairs (Psa. xxxiii. 12-22; xliv. 1-3), evening (Psa. cxxi. 4-8) morning (Psa. iii. 5; v. 3) the Sabbath (Rev. i. 10-20) so of business, meals, journeys, rocks, storms, &c., &c.

(6.) Read the Bible with **biographical centres?** As it is of intensest interest to read Revolutionary history, with Washington as the centre, so it will be found pleasant to read Jewish and Christian history with Moses or Samuel, or Peter or Paul as a living centre, grouping the scenes of which they were the most prominent human figures around their personal histories.

(7.) Read and study the Bible **socially.** This is done in Teachers' Meetings, Bible Classes, &c. Each one's views are sure to be somewhat corrected, supplemented and stimulated by the views, arguments and suggestions of others.

(8.) Read the Bible comprehensively, getting the grand view of each book or set of books. This is hardly second in value to any method of Bible study, and yet is probably least followed of any. Bible reading is for the most part, either "in course" or with sharp analysis of single verses here and there, or in single chapters. It is of the highest importance that we should also get a a comprehensive bird's-eye view of each Bible epistle, each history, each biography, by reading it continuously to the end, or at least with as few intervals and as short as if we were reading a modern letter, biography or history. Who would expect to comprehend the history of America by reading a few pages from Washington's administration, and then a few lines from Buchanan's, followed by a few words some days after from Munroe's times, and an extract from the year of Andrew Johnson's administration? And yet that is the way many read ancient Jewish history, and wonder at the difference in customs and morality which they find in the different pages, having caught no conception of Israel growing like other nations. In order to a full understanding of Jewish history, that line should be followed through the Bible with continuous and comprehensive reading from its beginning to its close. So the biography of each Bible character should at one time be read in one or two sittings, and looked at as a whole, while at another time it may be important to read his single act and words analytically. It is important, on the same principle, to read a whole book of the Bible or a connected set of books continuously and comprehensively, to get the great general thought that pervades the whole. In illustration of this comprehensive reading of Bible books, we add a list of key words and key thoughts, which such a comprehensive reading has suggested. Other minds would perhaps see other central thoughts in some cases. We started out with the feeling that every book had some great purpose and leading thought, and that the author would usually frequently employ some characteristic word or phrase to express that thought which would be appropriately designated as the "key word" or "key words" of that book:—

Key Words of the Bible.

Genesis—"In the beginning GOD" (i. 1). *Exodus*—"Brought out of bondage by the hand of God" (viii. 19). *Leviticus*—"Redeemed" by sacrifice and priesthood. *Numbers*—God dealing with Israel as with "Sons." *Deuteronomy*—"Remember." *Joshua*—Inheriting the promises (xxiii. 14, 15). *Judges*—"Deliverer." *Ruth*—Godly households. 1 *Samuel*—"Thy God helpeth thee." 2 *Samuel*—"Thou lovest thine enemies" (xix. 6; xxiv. 10). *Kings and Chronicles*—"As long as he sought the Lord, God made him to prosper" (2 Chron. xxvi. 5.) *Ezra*—"Separate" (x. 11). *Nehemiah*—"Let us rise up and build." *Esther*—The man whom THE KING delighteth to honour. *Job*—(Type of the race history)

"GOD blessed the latter end of Job more than the beginning" (xlii. 12). *Psalms*—"Praise." *Proverbs*—"Wisdom." *Ecclesiastes*—"Vanity." *Song of Solomon*—"MY BELOVED." *Isaiah*—"Salvation." *Jeremiah*—"My hope in the day of evil" (xvii. 17). *Daniel*—"Kingdom" (vii. 27). *Hosea*—"Return" (iii. 5). *Joel*—"Deliverance" (ii. 32). *Amos*—"Seek ye ME" (v. 4). *Jonah*—"Angry" (i. 2, 4; iv. 4). *Micah*—"Many nations shall come" (iv. 2). *Nahum*—"Devoured" (i. 10). *Habakkuk*—"Woe" (ii. 12). *Zephaniah*—"Punish" (i. 12). *Haggai*—"Consider your ways" (i. 5). *Zechariah*—"Light" (xiv. 7). *Malachi*—"My Messenger" (iii. 1). *Matthew*—"Fulfilled" (i. 22) *Mark*—"Immediately." *Luke*—"Son of Man." *John*—"Believe" (xx. 31). *Acts*—"Power of Jesus's name" (iv. 10). *Romans*—"Judgment" and "Justification" (v. 18). *1 Corinthians*—"Let all your things be done with charity" (xvi. 14). *2 Corinthians*—"Our sufficiency" (iii. 5). *Galatians*—"The liberty of Sonship" (iv. 7). *Ephesians*—"Walk." *Philippians*—"The work of God in the heart perfected." *Colossians*—"Christ in you," *Letters to Thessalonians*—"Comfort" (1 Thess. iv. 8). *Letters to Timothy*—"The Doctrine which is according to Godliness" (x. 3). *Titus*—"Savior." *Philemon*—"Brother." *Hebrews*—"Better." *James*—"Work." *Letters of Peter*—"Precious." *1 John*—"Know." *2 and 3 John*—"The Truth." *Jude*—"Ungodly." *Revelation*—"Overcome."

The time required to read the individual books of the Bible is much less than is usually supposed. Genesis, which is the longest historical book in the Bible, can be read without haste, in three hours—an amount of time which almost every one frequently gives to a favorite author, at one or two sittings. Luke is the only New Testament book that requires two hours for its reading. Forty-two out of the sixty-six books of the Bible, may be read in less than an hour each. Of course, such books as Proverbs and Psalms, which have no continuous narrative, should not be read so continuously. The whole Bible, read as slowly as ordinary Scripture reading in the pulpit, would require only sixty hours and forty-eight minutes, the working hours of one week, equal to ten minutes a day for one year. Of course it would be best to scatter the week's time over the year, getting a comprehensive view of the whole Bible in one twelvemonth, and afterwards, of course, reading more slowly and analytically. It would make such a year plan more profitable and pleasant, if a whole Church, or a whole class tried the plan together, agreeing to read the same books at the same time, and giving ten minutes of each day to this delightful pursuit of truth.

To show that this comprehensive reading of the Scriptures is not impracticable, even for the busiest people, we subjoin a table showing the time required for thoughtful reading of each book of the Bible in hours and minutes:—

Time Required for Reading

THE BOOKS OF THE OLD TESTAMENT.

Book	Time	Book	Time	Book	Time
GENESIS	3.05	II. CHRONICLES	2.00	DANIEL	.35
EXODUS	2.30	EZRA	.50	HOSEA	.25
LEVITICUS	1.50	NEHEMIAH	.55	JOEL	.10
NUMBERS	1.45	ESTHER	.30	AMOS	.20
DEUTERONOMY	2.15	JOB	1.25	OBADIAH	.05
JOSHUA	1.25	PSALMS	3.35	JONAH	.05
JUDGES	1.20	PROVERBS	1.10	MICAH	.15
RUTH	.15	ECCLESIASTES	.27	NAHUM	.05
I. SAMUEL	1.50	SONG OF SOLOMON	.15	HABAKKUK	.07
II. SAMUEL	1.30	ISAIAH	2.50	ZEPHANIAH	.08
I. KINGS	1.50	JEREMIAH	3.15	HAGGAI	.05
II. KINGS	1.05	LAMENTATIONS	.17	ZECHARIAH	.30
I. CHRONICLES	1.40	EZEKIEL	3.00	MALACHI	.03

THE BOOKS OF THE NEW TESTAMENT.

Book	Time	Book	Time	Book	Time
MATTHEW	1.55	EPHESIANS	.17	HEBREWS	.35
MARK	1.10	PHILLIPPIANS	.12	JAMES	.12
LUKE	2.00	COLOSSIANS	.15	I. PETER	.14
JOHN	1.30	I. THESSALONIANS	.10	II. PETER	.10
THE ACTS	1.55	II THESSALONIANS	.06	I. JOHN	.13
ROMANS	.45	I. TIMOTHY	.13	II. JOHN	.02
I. CORINTHIANS	.43	II TIMOTHY	.10	III. JOHN	.02
II. CORINTHIANS	.23	TITUS	.05	JUDE	.04
GALATIANS	.17	PHILEMON	.03	REVELATION	.50

Let it be remembered in this and every method of Bible reading, that "*the letter killeth*, THE SPIRIT GIVETH LIFE."

"TEN MINUTES A DAY" PLAN FOR COMPREHENSIVE READING OF THE WHOLE BIBLE IN ONE YEAR.

JANUARY: ... ... Proverbs, Genesis, and Revelation. Total, 5 hours, 5 minutes.
FEBRUARY: ... ... Ezekiel. Total, 3 hours. (But should be read more slowly, or twice over.)
MARCH: ... ... Exodus, Galatians, and Philemon; Leviticus and Hebrews. Total, 4 hours, 35 minutes.
APRIL: ... ... Numbers, Ephesians, 2 John, 3 John, Deuteronomy, Romans, and James. Total, 4 hours, 38 minutes.
MAY: ... . Joshua, 2 Corinthians and Titus; Judges, Hosea, 1 Corinthians, and Ezra. Total, 4 hours, 31 minutes.
JUNE: ... ... Ruth, Luke,* Acts, and Daniel. Total, 4 hours, 25 minutes.
JULY AND AUGUST: 1 Samuel, 2 Samuel, Psalms,† 1 Kings, 2 Kings. Total, 9 hours, 10 minutes.

---

* At some time in one's life he should get a harmony of the Gospels, and read through the life of Christ, as you would read a biography of Wesley or Luther. In such a reading Christ's teachings take on new aspects, and the life itself assumes a new significance.

† David's Psalms are his autobiography, and ought to be read in connection with his biography in Samuel, in order to get his complete history from both the outward and inward points of view. The Psalms will be tenfold more significant if read with the events that suggested them, and the bare outline of David's public history will be shaded and tinted into life-like distinctness and completeness by inserting at appropriate places these heart-chapters of historic song. I have accordingly arranged the Psalms of David in their probable historic connection, as given by the best biblical scholars, or shown by the titles or contents.

1. David's shepherd life—1 Sam. 16. Psalms 19, 23.
2. David's victory over Goliath—1 Sam. 17, 18. Psalms 8, 9.
3. Saul's effort to capture David in his own home—1 Sam. 19:11. Psalm 59.
4. Jonathan's warning—1 Sam. 20:35-42. Psalms 11, 64.
5. David's flight to Ahimelech, the priest—1 Sam. 21:1-9, etc. Psalm 52.
6. David's flight to Gath—1 Sam. 21:11. Psalms 56, 70.
7. Escape from Gath—1 Sam. 22:1. Psalm 34.
8. David in the cave of Adullam—1 Sam. 21:1, 2. Psalms 57, 142, 13, 40, 141.
9. In the forest of Hareth—1 Sam. 22:5; 23:14, 16. Psalms 63, 17.
10. Escape from Keilah to mountains of Ziph—1 Sam. 23:10-13. Psalms 31, 54.
11. David sparing Saul—1 Sam. 24:1-16. Psalm 7. (An appeal against Cush who had slandered him to Saul, saying, "David seeketh thy hurt.")
12. The cave of Engedi—1 Sam. 23:29. Psalms 35, 36.
13. Wilderness of Paran,—Incident of Nabal—1 Sam. 25. Psalm 53. [Nabal means "fool."]
14. Ziklag—1 Sam. 27. Psalms 16, 33, 39.
15. David, king at Hebron—2 Sam. 2:1-7. Psalms 26, 101.

SEPTEMBER:	Joel, Amos, Obadiah, Jonah, Nahum, Habakkuk, Zephaniah, Haggai, Malachi, 1 Chronicles, 2 Chronicles, and Esther. Total, 4 hours, 43 minutes.
OCTOBER:	Ecclesiastes, Isaiah, John, and Canticles. Total, 4 hours, 22 minutes.
NOVEMBER:	Jeremiah, Lamentations, Zechariah, and Mark. Total, 5 hours, 12 minutes.
DECEMBER:	Job, Jude, Micah, and Matthew; 1 Thessalonians, 2 Thessalonians; 1 Peter and 2 Peter; Nehemiah, 1 Timothy and 2 Timothy; Colossians, Philippians, and 1 John. Total, 4 hours, 57 minutes.

7. TOPICAL BIBLE READING.

BY. D. L. MOODY.

IN order to understand the Bible we have to study it carefully. If we will go to the Word of God and be willing to be taught by the Holy Ghost, God will teach us, and will unfold His blessed truths to us.

---

16. King at Jerusalem—2 Sam. 5: 6-25. Psalms 21, 108, 110.
17. The Ark brought to Jerusalem—2 Sam. 7. Psalms 132, 15, 24, 94, 138, 29.
18. Wars of David with Edom, Syria, etc.—2 Sam. 8. Psalms 60, 61, 44, 20.
19. David's penitence for the "great transgression."—2 Sam. 11, etc. Psalms 51, 32, 6, 69, 103.
20. Absalom's rebellion—2 Sam. 15-18. Psalms 4, (first evening of flight); 3 (next morning; also the two Psalms next mentioned), 5, 143, 26, 28, 61, 144, 62, 143, 42.
21. Ahithophel's treason—2 Sam. 15-18. Psalms 55, 41, 109.
22. Victory over Absalom—2 Sam. 18. Psalm 43. (David's prayer at Mahanaim, while Joab fought with Absalom in the woods.)
23. Sheba's rebellion—2 Sam. 20, 21. Psalms 2, 84.
24. David's review of his many victories—2 Sam. 22. Psalm 18.
25. The pestilence withdrawn—1 Chron. 20: 14-30; 21: 1. Psalm 30.
26. The Building of the Temple committed to Solomon—1 Chron. 28, etc. Psalms 65, 67, 68.
27. David's review of his life—Psalm 145.
28. Giving the kingdom to Solomon—1 Chron. 29. Psalms 72, 91.

The authorities chiefly consulted in this arrangement, are Lange's Commentary, Dr. Wm. M. Taylor's David, King of Israel, and a book by the Rev. Henry Linton, of England, on The Psalms of David and Solomon.

There are **three books that every Christian ought to have** if he cannot have but three. The first is a Bible—one with good plain print that you can easily read, not so good that you are afraid to mark it. I am sick of these little fine types. It is a good thing to get a good-sized Bible, because you will grow old by-and-by, and your sight may grow poor, and you won't want to give up the one you have been used to reading in after it has come to seem like a sort of life-long companion. The next book to get is "Cruden's Concordance." You cannot get on very well in Bible study without that. There is another book printed in this country by the American Tract Society called the "Bible Text-Book." It was brought out first in London. These three books will be a wonderful help to you in studying the Word of God.

For a number of years I have made a rule not to read any book that does not help me to understand the Bible. I am a greater slave to that book than any man is to strong drink, and I am sure it does me a great deal more good. I think I have got **the key to the study of the Bible. Take it topically!** Take "Love," for instance, and spend a month in searching what the Bible says about love, from Genesis to Revelation. Thus you will learn to love everybody, whether they love you or not. In the same way, take "Grace," "Faith," "Assurance," "Heaven," and so on. When you read your Bible, be sure you *hunt for something.* Read the same chapter over and over again, till you understand it. I would add—Make yourself thoroughly familiar with Paul's Epistles. They are the key to all the Holy Scriptures. Get a reference Bible, and you will find the best commentary in the margin.

Take up one word in a book, such as the "*believes*" in St. John. Every chapter but two, speaks of believing. Look up the nineteen personal interviews with Christ. Take the "*conversions*" of the Bible: the seven "*blesseds*" and "*overcomes*" of Revelation. See what 1 John iii. says about "*assurance,*" and the six things worth "*knowing.*" Take up the five "*precious*" things of Peter, the "*verilys*" of John, the seven "*walks*" of Ephesians, the four "*much mores*" of Rom. iv., the two "*receiveds*" of John i., the seven "*hearts*" in Prov. xxiii., and especially an eighth, the "*lookings,*" the "*lookings back,*" the "*beholds*" of the Bible.

Study the word in God's presence, with the help of the asked-for Spirit of God. If you have sin upon your conscience, it will hinder your understanding. Remember the blood. The light which shines from Calvary is the light that unfolds the Scriptures.

In order to aid in topical "Bible Readings" for private edification as well as for public use we add Bagster's "Scripture Index," from the famous "Bagster Bible," every topic of which would make a profitable "Bible Reading."

Extracts from Bagster's Scripture Index,
In Bagster's Polyglot Bible.

ACCESS TO GOD.

The typical way—Heb. 9. 6–8. Lev. chapters 1–9, and 16, 21, 22.
The new and living way—John 14. 6. Ro. 5. 1, 2. Eph. 2. 13, 18; 3. 11, 12. Heb. 9. 24.
Exhortation—Heb. 4. 14, 15 : 10. 19–22. Matt. 11. 28. 1 Pet. 2. 4, 5.
Promises—Jno. 6. 37. Jas. 4. 8.

ADOPTION.

Natural—Ex. 2. 10. Est. 2. 7.
Spiritual—Jno. 1. 12, 13. 1 Jno. 3. 1, 2. Rom. 8, 14, 15. Gal. 3. 7, 26; 4. 4–7. Rom. 8. 16, 17. Eph. 1. 4, 5. Heb. 2. 11. Rom. 8. 22, 23.
Promises—Ps. 34. 11. Jer. 31. 9. 2 Co. 6. 18.
Exhortation—1 Jno. 3. 9, 10. 1 Pet. 1. 22, 23. Heb. 12. 9, 10. 2 Co. 6. 17. Phil. 2. 14, 15. Eph. 5. 1.

AFFLICTION.

From God—Ex. 4. 11. Job 1. 12; 2. 6. Ps. 66. 10, 11. Amos 3. 6. 2 Co. 12. 7. Is. 53. 10. Acts 4. 27, 28.
Common to all—Gen. 3. 16, 17. Job 5. 6, 7. Luke 13. 2.
Special to some—2 Tim. 3. 12. Jno. 16. 33. Heb. 12. 6, 7. Rev. 3. 19. Jno. 15. 2. Acts 14. 22. 1 Co. 11. 32; 7. 28.
Uses of—Ps. 119. 71. 67. Jno. 9. 2, 3; 11. 4. Is. 26. 9. Hos. 5. 15. Ps. 78. 34. Luke 15. 17–19. Deut. 8. 5, 16. 1 Co. 11. 32. 2 Co. 4. 17, 18. Heb. 12. 11. Jas. 1. 2, 3. 1 Pet. 1. 7; 4. 12–14. Rev. 2. 10.

ALMS-GIVING.

Directions for—2 Co. 9. 7. 1 Co. 16. 2. Deut. 15. 7, 8. Lu. 3. 11; 11. 41. Eph. 4. 28. 1 Tim. 6. 17, 18. Heb. 13. 16. 1 Jno. 3. 17. Gal. 6. 16.
Promises—Ps. 41. 1; 112. 9. Prov. 14. 21; 19. 17; 28. 27. Matt. 25. 31–40. Lu. 6. 38; 14. 13, 14. Heb. 6. 10.
Warnings—Prov. 21. 13. Eze. 18. 12, 13. Matt. 25. 41–46; 6. 1, 3. 1 Co. 13. 3.

ANGELS.

Their Ministry—Heb. 1. 14. Gen. 19. 1–15. Dan. 9. 21, 22; 10. 18, 19. Lu. 2. 10; 15. 10. Matt. 4. 11. Lu. 22. 43. Matt. 28. 2; 13 41. 1 Thess. 4. 16.
Their number—Rev. 5. 11. Heb. 12. 22.

ANOINTING.

Typical—Ex. 28. 41; 29. 7; 40. 15; 40. 9–11; 30. 31, 32.
Spiritual—Heb. 1. 8, 9. 2 Co. 1. 21, 22. 1 Jno. 2 20, 27.

APOSTACY.

Of angels—Jude 6.
Of man—Gen. 3. 6.
Of Israel—Ex. 32. 7, 8. Is. 1. 4–6.
Of disciples—Jno. 6. 66
Of the latter days—1 Tim. 4. 1–3.

ASCENSION, THE

Mar. 16. 19. Lu. 24. 51. Acts 1. 9–11.
Typified—Lev. 14. 4–7.
Foretold—Ps. 63. 18. Jno. 6. 62; 7. 3 14. 28; 16. 5; 20. 17.

Necessity—Jno. 16. 7.
Its object—Ro. 8. 34. Heb. 9. 24. Jno. 14 2.
Its result—Acts 2. 32, 33. Eph. 2. 4–7.

ASSURANCE.

Of Sonship—Heb. 3. 14. Ro. 8. 16. 1 Jno. 3. 2.
Of eternal Life—1 Jno. 3. 14. Jno. 10. 28, 29.
Of abiding union with Christ—Jno. 17. 24. Rom. 8. 38, 39.

ATONEMENT.

Is of God—Zec. 13. 7–9. Isa. 53. 10. Jno. 3. 16.
Through love—1 Jno. 4. 10. Rom. 5. 8; 8. 32. 2 Co. 5. 18, 19.
How accomplished—Lev. 17. 11. Heb. 9. 22. Eph. 1. 6, 7. Col. 1. 14. 1 Jno. 1. 7. Rev. 7. 14; 12. 11.
Its result—Heb. 2. 9. Isa. 53. 5, 6. 1 Pet. 2. 24. Jno. 1. 29. Ro. 5. 10, 11; 3. 24, 25. Gal. 1. 3, 4. Ro. 5. 9. Heb. 10. 14. 1 Thess. 1. 10. Heb. 9. 28.

BAPTISM.

Of water by John—Matt. 3. 11–15. Mar. 1. 4. Matt. 3. 5, 6. Mar. 1. 8, 9. Lu. 3. 12; 7. 29. Matt. 3. 7. Lu. 7. 30.
Of fire—Mar. 10. 38, 39. Lu. 12. 49, 51. Matt. 3. 11.
Of the Holy Ghost—Matt. 3. 11–16. Acts 1. 5; 2. 1–4; 8. 14–17; 10, 36–38, 44; 18. 24, 25; 19. 1–6.
In the name of the Lord Jesus—Acts 2. 28, 41. Acts 8. 12–17, 36–38; 9. 17, 18; 22. 16; 10. 44–48.
In the name of the Trinity—Matt. 28. 18, 19.
Its symbolical character—1 Co. 12. 12–14, 27. Eph. 4. 3–5. Ro. 6. 3, 4. Col. 2. 9–13.

BLINDNESS.

Typical—Lev. 21. 18, 21; 22. 22. Deut. 15. 21. Mal. 1. 8.
Spiritual—Jer. 5. 21. Is. 44. 18; 29. 10, 11; 6. 9, 10. Judg. 16. 20. Is. 1. 3. Ro. 11. 25. 2 Co. 3. 14, 15.
Of the natural man—1 Co. 2. 14. 2 Co. 4. 3, 4. Jno. 14. 17. Acts 26. 17, 18. Eph. 4. 17, 18.
Exhortation—Eph. 5. 8. 2 Pet. 1. 9, 10. 1 Jno. 1. 5, 6; 2. 9, 11. Rev. 3. 17, 18.

BLOOD.

Typical—Ex. 12. 13; 23. 18. Heb. 9. 22.
Of Christ—1 Jno. 5. 6, 8. Matt. 26. 28. Mar. 14. 24. Lu. 22. 20. Jno. 6. 53–56. 1 Co. 10. 16; 11. 25.

Effects of—Eph. 1. 7. Col. 1. 14. 1 Pet. 1. 18, 19. Rev. 5. 9. Col. 1. 20. Ro. 5. 9. Rev. 1. 5. Eph. 2. 13. 1 Jno. 1. 7. Rev. 7. 14. Heb. 9. 13, 14; 10. 19; 13. 12, 20, 21. Rev. 12. 11.
Exhortation—Acts 20. 28. 1 Co. 5. 7, 8.

CHARITY OR LOVE.

Characterized—1 Co. 13. 1–8; 8. 1; 13. 13.
Exhortation—1 Pet. 4. 8. 1 Tim. 1. 5. Col. 3. 14. 1 Co. 16. 14.

CHILDREN

Of God.
  By nature—Eph. 2. 3.
  By faith—Gal. 3. 26. 1 Jno. 5. 1. Jno. 1. 11, 12.
  Their true sonship—Gal. 4. 4–7. 1 Jno. 3. 1, 2. Ro. 8. 14, 16.
Exhortation to separateness—1 Jno. 3. 9, 10. 2 Co. 6. 17, 18.
To growth—1 Co. 14. 20. Heb. 5. 12–14. Eph. 4. 14, 15.
Of men.
Training of—Deut. 4. 9; 6. 7; 21. 18–21. Prov. 13. 24; 19. 18; 23. 13, 14; 20. 15, 17; 22. 6. Lam. 3. 27.
Duties of—Ex. 20. 12. Lev. 19. 3. Eph. 6. 1–3. 1 Tim. 5. 4, 8, 16.
Exhortation—Ec. 12. 1. Prov. 3. 1; 5. 1; 6. 20; 23. 22. Col. 3. 20.
Promises—Prov. 8. 17. Isa. 40. 11. Acts 2. 39.
Of the Devil—Jno. 8. 44. Matt. 23. 15. 1 Jno. 3. 10. Acts 13. 10. Jno. 6. 70.

COMMUNION.

With the Father—1 Jno. 1. 3, 7. Jno. 14. 23.
With the Son—1 Co. 1. 9. 1 Jno. 1. 3. Phil. 3. 10. Rev. 3. 20.
With the Spirit—2 Co. 13. 14. 1 Co. 12. 13. Phil. 2. 1, 2.
Necessary to a godly walk—Amos 3. 3.
Warnings—2 Co. 6. 14. 1 Jno. 1. 6. Heb. 13. 14.

CONFESSION OF SIN.

Under Law—Jos. 7. 19, 20, 25.
Under Grace—1 Jno. 1. 9. Jas. 5. 16.
Personal—Lev. 5. 1, 5. Prov. 28. 13. Ps. 32. 5. Num. 5. 6, 7.
Israel's sin—Lev. 16. 21; 26. 40, 42. Ezra 10. 11. Dan. 9. 20, 21.
Examples—Num. 21. 7. 1 Sa. 7. 6. 1 Sa. 12. 19. 2 Sa. 24. 10. Job 7. 20. Dan. 9. 4, 5. Lu. 23. 41.

CONSCIENCE.

Job 33. 14, 15, 16. Gen. 3. 9, 10, 11; 4

9 ; 42. 21. Ex. 20. 19. Num. 17, 12, 13.
Jno. 8, 7, 9. Acts 24. 25.
A weak conscience—Ro. 14. 2, 5, 6. 1 Co.
8. 7. 1 Tim. 4. 4. Ro. 14. 14. 1 Co. 8.
12 ; 10. 28, 29. Ro. 14. 22. Tit. 1. 15.
A good conscience—Acts 23. 1. 2 Tim. 1.
3. Acts 24. 16. Ro. 9. 1. 1 Co. 4. 4. 1
Tim. 1, 19. 1 Pet. 3. 16, 21.
A purged conscience—Heb. 9. 8, 9, 14 ;
10. 2.
An evil conscience—1 Tim. 4. 1, 2. Tit.
1. 15.

CONVERSION.

How wrought—Isa. 55. 6, 7. Eze. 33. 11 ;
36. 25-28.
Indispensable—Matt. 18, 3.
By the Father—Jno. 6. 44, 37.
By the Son—Jno. 14. 6.
By the Holy Ghost—1 Co. 12. 3.
A Promise—Jas. 5. 19, 20.
An Exhortation—Lu. 22, 32.

COVENANT.

With Noah—Gen. 6. 18 ; 9. 13-15 ; 8. 21,
22.
With Abraham—Gen. 12. 1-3 ; 13. 14-16 ;
15. 18 ; 17. 20, 21 ; 22. 16-18.
Of Circumcision—Gen. 17. 1, 2, 10, 13, 14.
With Isaac—Gen. 26. 4.
With Jacob—Gen. 28. 13, 14,
At Horeb—Deut. 5. 2, 3. Ex. 19. 5, 8.
In Christ—Gal. 3. 17. Acts 15. 5, 10, 22,
28, 29. 2 Co. 3. 6-8.
A new covenant—Jer. 31. 31-33. Heb. 8.
7, 8, 13. 16. Ro. 6. 14 ; 11. 23, 25-27.
Heb. 7. 11, 12, 22. Ro. 11. 26, 27. 2 Co.
3. 14. Heb. 9. 15. Rev. 13, 8. 1 Pet. 1.
20. Heb. 13. 20, 21.

CROSS, THE.

Its type—Num. 21. 8, 9. Jno. 3. 14, 15 ;
12. 32, 33.
Its result to Jew and Gentile—Eph. 2. 16.
Its result to the Church of God—Gal. 2.
20 ; 5. 24. Col. 3. 3, 4.
Its result to the World—1 Co. 1. 18-24.
Enmity to—Phil. 3. 18, 19.

DEATH.

Appointed unto men—Gen. 3. 17, 19. Ro.
5. 12. Heb. 9. 27, 28. Isa. 40. 6, 7. 1
Pet. 1. 24.
Exceptions—Heb. 11. 5. 2 Ki. 2. 11. Jno.
11. 26. 1 Co. 15. 51. 1 Thess. 4. 17.
How abolished—1 Co. 15. 22, 26, 54, 56.
Heb. 2. 14. Rev. 21. 4.
Union with Christ—Ro. 8, 38, 39. 1 Co.
3. 21-23.
The second Death—Rev. 20. 14 ; 21. 8 ;
Rev. 2. 11.

Exhortation—Ps. 90. 10, 12. Ec. 9. 10.
Matt. 10. 28. Eze. 33. 11. 2 Co. 4. 11,
16. Lu. 12. 19-21. Ro. 6. 23. Jno. 5.
24.
Death of the Soul—Matt. 10. 28.
Warnings—Dan. 12. 2. Pro. 14. 12. Matt.
7. 13. Ro. 8, 13. Rev. 3. 1.

DEVIL.

Rev. 12, 9.
In Eden—Gen. 3. 1, 13-15.
As God of this World—2 Co. 4. 4. Eph. 2.
2. Jno. 14. 20. Matt. 13, 38, 39. 1
Chron. 21. 1. Zec. 3. 1. Job 1. 6, 7 ;
2. 1, 2. 1 Pet. 5. 8. Rev. 2. 10.
His power limited—Job 2. 6. 1 Co. 5. 5.
Matt. 4. 3, 5, 8, 9.
His overthrow—2 Tim. 2. 25, 26. 1 Jno.
3, 8. Heb. 2. 14. Rev. 12. 9, 10 ; 20. 2,
7, 9. 10.

FAITH.

Heb. 11. 1. Ro. 8. 24, 25. 1 Co. 13. 12,
13. Ro. 10. 17.
All-important—Heb. 11. 6. Eph. 6. 16. 1
Thess. 5. 8. Heb. 4. 2.
Its operation—Jno. 1. 12. 1 Jno. 5. 1.
Rom. 1. 16, 17. Heb. 11. 3. Gal. 3. 6.
Ro. 4. 5 ; 3. 28. Acts 10. 43. Eph. 3.
17-19 ; 2. 8. 1 Pet. 1. 8, 9. Ro. 5. 1.
Heb. 4. 1-3. Gal. 1. 20. Ro. 5. 2. Jno
3. 16. 1 Jno. 5. 4, 5.
The gift of God—Eph. 2. 8. Ro. 12. 3.
1 Co. 12. 8, 9. Jno. 12. 39, 40. 1 Tim.
4. 10.
Examples—Heb. 11.
Exhortation—Ps. 34. 8 ; 37. 5. Matt. 6.
25. Jno. 12. 36. Ro. 11. 20, 21. 1 Tim.
6. 12. Heb. 10. 35, 38. Jno. 20. 27.
Promises—Ps. 55. 22. Isa. 26. 3, 4 ; 30. 15.
2 Tim. 4. 7, 8. Mar. 9. 23 ; 11. 24. 1
Jno. 5. 14.

FALL, THE.

Gen. 2. 16, 17 ; 3. 6. Ro. 5. 12. Job 14.
4.
The remedy—Ro. 5. 19-21. 1 Co 15. 22,
47-49.
Warning—2 Co. 11. 3.

FORGIVENESS.

How obtained—1 Jno. 1. 9. Isa. 43. 25.
Ps. 25, 11. Heb. 9. 22. 2 Co. 5. 18, 19.
Isa. 53. 4, 5. 2 Co. 5. 51. 1 Pet. 2. 24.
Heb. 9. 26-28. Ro. 4. 6-8. Acts 5. 30,
31 ; 10. 43.
Already bestowed—Eph. 1. 7. Col. 1. 14 ;
2. 13. 1 Jno. 2. 12. Heb. 10. 1, 2.
Exhortation—Matt. 6. 14, 15. Mar. 11. 25,
26. Lu. 17. 3, 4. Matt. 18. 21, 22. Jas
2. 12, 13. Col. 3. 12, 13. Eph. 4. 32.

GOSPEL, THE.

Ro. 1. 16, 17 ; 10. 3, 6, 9, 10 ; 11. 6 ; 3. 21, 22, 31. Mar. 16. 15, 16.
Exhortation—Eph. 6. 15. Phil. 1. 27. 1 Pet. 4. 17.
Promises—Mar. 10. 29, 30 ; 8. 35.

HEAVEN.

Isa. 66. 1. Job 15. 15. Jno 3. 13 ; 14. 2. Heb. 11. 14, 16. 1 Pet. 1. 3, 4. Acts 3. 21 ; 1. 11.
Opened—Matt. 3. 16. Jno. 1. 51. Acts 7. 56. Rev. 19. 11.
New Heavens—2 Pet. 3. 13. Rev. 21. 1.
Paradise—Gen. 5. 24. 2 Ki. 2. 11. Lu. 16. 22 ; 23. 43. 2 Co. 12. 4. Acts 2. 33, 34.

HOLY SPIRIT.

Creator—Gen. 1. 2. Ps. 33. 6. Job 26. 13.
The Comforter—Jno. 16. 7 ; 14. 16, 17 ; 7. 39. 1 Jno. 3. 24 ; 4. 13. Lu. 24. 49. Acts 1. 4, 5 ; 2. 1-4, 32, 33 ; 4. 31 ; 8. 17 ; 2. 38 ; 10. 44, 45. Jno. 15. 26 ; 16. 13, 14. 2 Co. 1. 22. Gal. 4. 6. Lu. 11. 13.
His operation—2 Pet. 1. 21, 22. Lu. 1. 67, 68, 70. 2 Sam. 23. 2. Mar. 12. 36. Lu. 1. 35. Matt. 1. 18, 20. Jno. 1. 32, 33. Lu. 4. 1. Heb. 9. 14. 1 Pet. 3. 18. Acts 13. 2, 4. Eph. 2. 18. Acts 16. 6, 7. Ro. 8. 26, 27. 1 Co. 12. 3. Jno. 3. 5, 6. Eph. 1. 13, 14.
Fruit of—Gal. 5. 5, 22, 23. Ro. 14. 17 ; 15. 13.
Exhortation—2 Tim. 1. 6, 7. Eph. 4. 30. Acts 20. 28. Gal. 5. 16-18. Ro. 8. 2, 5, etc. Gal. 5. 25.
Warnings—Acts 5. 3, 9 ; 7. 51 ; 28. 25, 26. 1 Co. 2. 14 ; 3. 16, 17 ; 6. 19. Jno. 6. 63. Eph. 4. 30. Mar. 3. 29. 1 Thess. 5. 19.

HUMILITY.

Gal. 6. 3. Phil. 2. 3.
Not natural to man—Mar. 7. 21, 22. 1 Co. 4. 6, 7 ; 3. 18. 1 Jno. 2. 16.
Our example—Matt. 11. 29. Lu. 2. 51. Phil. 2. 7, 8.
Exhortation—Ro. 12. 3 ; 16. 19. Isa. 10. 15. Col. 3. 12.
Warnings—Pro. 15. 33. Ro. 11. 20, 21. Ps. 10. 4. Pro. 26. 12. 1 Co. 10. 12.
Encouragement—Isa. 57. 15. Jas. 4. 6. 1 Pet. 5. 6.

JESUS CHRIST.

His divinity—Col. 2. 9. 1 Tim. 3. 16. Jno. 1. 1, 14, 18. Col. 1. 15-19. 1 Co. 15. 47. Heb. 1. 2, 3. 1 Co. 2. 8. Jno. 1. 3 ; 10, 30, 36 ; 14. 8, 9. 10, 13,14. Phil. 2. 6, 10, 11. Isa. 45. 21-23.
His incarnation—Heb. 2. 16. Gal. 4. 4, 5. Isa. 7: 14 ; 9. 6. Heb. 9. 26: Matt. 1. 18.
His life as Son of Abraham—Gospel of Matthew.
His life as perfect Servant and Sacrifice—Gospel of Mark.
His life as Son of Man—Gospel of Luke.
His life as Son of God—Gospel of John.
His Baptism—Lu. 3. 21, 22.
His Temptation—Lu. 4. 1, 2. Mar. 1. 12. 13. Heb. 4. 15.
His Death—Heb. 9. 14.
His Resurrection—1 Pet. 3. 18.
His Ascension—Acts 1. 9. Lu. 24. 51.
His Mediation—1 Tim. 2. 5. Heb. 9. 24 ; 7. 25. Ro. 8. 34. 1 Jno. 2. 1.
His Coming again—Acts 1. 11. Mark 14. 62. 1 Thess. 4. 16, 17. Mar. 13. 25, 26. Matt. 24. 30. Mar. 8. 38. 2 Thess. 1. 7, 8, 10. Rev. 22. 20.

JUDGMENT.

Day of—Rev. 22. 12. Ecc. 12. 14. Matt. 12. 36. 25. 31, 32. Rev. 11. 18 ; 20. 12 ; 14. 6.
The Judge—Jno. 5. 22, 27 ; 12. 48. Matt. 7. 22, 23. Ro. 14. 10, 12. 2 Tim. 4. 1, 8. Acts 10. 42 ; 17. 31. Matt. 13. 41, 42.
Exhortation—2 Pet. 3. 7, 10, 14. 1 Pet. 4. 17. Jude 14, 15. Jno. 3. 18, 19.

JUSTIFICATION.

1 Co. 6. 9-11.
Who are Justified—Ro. 2. 13 ; 3. 20. Ps. 14. 3. 2.
How obtained—Ro. 8. 3-5. 2 Co. 5. 21. Jas. 2. 21. Ro. 4. 2. Gal. 3. 11, 24 ; 2. 16. Isa. 53. 11. Ro. 3. 24-26. Tit. 3. 5-7. Ro. 11. 6.

KINGDOM OF GOD.—KINGDOM OF HEAVEN.

To be sought for—Matt. 6. 33. Lu. 12. 31. Matt. 6. 9, 10. Luke 11. 2.
Its nature—Jno. 18. 36. Lu. 17. 21. 1 Co. 4. 20. Lu. 18. 29, 30. Ro. 14. 17.
Hidden to some—Matt. 13. 11. Mar. 4. 11. Lu. 8. 10.
Its approach—Lu. 17. 20. Matt. 24. 14. Lu. 19. 11 ; 22. 16, 18. Matt. 26. 29. Mar. 14. 25. Matt. 21. 31.
Who enter—Matt. 7. 21 ; 5. 19, 20 : 19. 24. Gal. 5. 19, 21. Eph. 5. 5. 1 Co. 6. 9, 10. Jas. 2. 5. Matt. 5. 3, 10. Lu. 10. 20. Mar. 10. 14, 15. Acts 14. 22. Matt. 16. 19.
Similitudes—Matt. chaps. 13. 18. 20. 22. 25. Mar. chap. 4. Lu. chaps. 13. 19, etc.
Warnings—Matt. 21. 43. Lu. 13. 28, 29. Matt. 8. 11, 12. Lu. 9. 62. Matt. 21. 31, 32 ; 18. 1-4. Jno. 3. 3, 5.
Exhortation—1 Thess. 2. 11, 12. 2 Pet. 1. 10, 11. Heb. 12. 28.

LIBERTY.

Jno. 8. 32, 36. 2 Co. 3. 17. Col. 2. 16, 20. Ro. 14. 5.
Exhortation—Gal. 5. 1, 13. 1 Pet. 2. 16. 1 Co. 8. 9.

LIFE.

Spiritual—Jno. 1. 12, 13. 1 Pet. 1. 3, 4. 1 Jno. 5. 1, 18. Col. 2. 13. Eph. 2. 4, 5. 1 Jno. 4. 9. 1 Pet. 1. 23. Jno. 6. 33. 1 Jno. 5. 12. Jno. 5. 21; 3. 3, 6.
Warning—Ro. 8. 8, 9.
Eternal—Ro. 6. 23. Jno. 3. 14–16; 17. 1–3; 3. 36. 1 Jno. 5. 11–13. Jno. 5. 24; 6. 47, 54.

LONG-SUFFERING.

2 Co. 5. 18–20. Ro. 2. 4. 2 Pet. 3. 9. Gen. 6. 3.
Warning—Ecc. 8. 11, 12.

OBEDIENCE.

1 Sa. 15. 22. Deut. 27. 26. Jas. 2. 10.
Of Christ—Ro. 5. 19. 1 Pet. 1. 2. 2 Co. 10. 5, 6. Jno. 8. 29.
Illustration—Ro. 6. 16, 17.
Exhortation—Jas. 1. 22–25. 1 Jno. 2. 4–6.

PARENTS.

Exhortation—Pro. 22. 6. Deut. 4. 9; 6. 7; 11. 18, 19. Joel 1. 3. Pro. 13. 24; 19. 18; 22. 15; 23. 13, 14. Heb. 12. 7. Eph. 6. 4. Col. 3. 21. Lu. 11. 13.
Warnings—Ex. 20. 5; 34. 7. Job 21. 19, (marg.) Isa. 14. 20–23. 1 Tim. 5. 8. Matt. 10. 37.

PATIENCE.

Phil. 4. 5. 1 Pet. 2. 20. Tit. 3. 2. 2 Tim. 2. 24. Ro. 12. 12. Jas. 3. 17. 1 Thess. 5. 14. Jas. 5. 7, 8.
Our example—Isa. 53. 7. 1 Pet. 2. 23.

PERSECUTION.

2 Tim. 3. 12. Jno. 16. 33. Phil. 1. 29.
The cause—Jno. 15. 18–21. Gal. 4. 28, 29. Gal. 5. 11.
The result—Lu. 6. 22, 23. 1 Pet. 4. 12–14. Rev. 7. 13–17; 20. 4–6.
The power to sustain—Heb. 12. 3. 2 Tim. 2. 12.
Exhortation—2 Tim. 1. 8. Heb. 13. 13. Matt. 5. 44, 45.

PRAISE.

Ps. 50. 23; 47. 6; 51. 15; 63. 3, 5, 6; 92. 1; 95. 1, 2. Heb. 13. 15. 1 Pet. 2. 9. Rev. 5. 12, 13; 19. 6, 7.

PRAYER.

Prov. 15. 8. Ps. 145. 18, 19. Jer. 29. 12, 13. Matt. 6. 6–13; 21. 22. Jno. 14. 13, 14; 15. 7, 16; 16. 23, 24. Jas. 5. 14, 15. Mar. 11. 24, 25. Ps. 81. 10. Matt. 18. 19. 1 Jno. 5. 14, 15; 3. 22.
For wisdom—Jas. 1. 5. Prov. 3. 5, 6.
For deliverance—Ps. 34. 15; 50. 15. Heb. 4. 16. Job 27. 8–10.
For guidance—Ps. 37. 5. Pro. 16. 3.
The Spirit's help—Ro. 8. 26. Eph. 2. 18; 6. 18. Jude 20. 21. Lu. 11. 13.
Exhortation—Mar. 14. 38. Jas. 5. 13. 1 Pet. 4. 7. Phil. 4. 6. Jno. 15. 7. 1 Jno. 3. 21, 22. Jas. 1. 6, 7.
Warnings—Heb. 11. 6. Matt. 6. 5. Jas. 4. 2, 3; 1. 5–7. Isa. 1. 15. Ps. 66. 18. Job 27. 8, 9. Matt. 17. 21. Prov. 28. 9. Jno. 9. 31.

PREACHING.

1 Co. 1. 21. Ro. 10. 14, 15. Tit. 1. 3.
The subject—1 Co. 1. 23, 24. 2 Co. 4. 5. Eph. 3. 8–10. Ro. 16. 25, 26. Gal. 1. 7–9. Phil. 1. 14–20. Lu. 24. 27. Acts 11. 20; 8. 5, 12, 35; 17. 2, 3, 18. Ro. 10. 8, 9.
The power—Acts 4. 13. 1 Co. 3. 6, 7. 2 Co. 3. 5, 6. Heb. 4. 2.
The manner—1 Co. 2. 4; 1. 17, 18; 3. 10, 11. Acts 5. 42. Mar. 16. 15, 20. Acts 10. 36, 40, 42. 2 Tim. 4. 1. 2.
The reward—1 Co. 9. 14, 18.

PRIDE.

1 Pet. 5. 5. Prov. 16. 5; 8. 13. Ps. 101. 5. Prov. 6. 16, 17.
Warnings—Lu. 11. 43. Prov. 15. 25; 16. 18, 19. Prov. 30. 12, 13. Mal. 4. 1. Matt. 23. 12.

REGENERATION.

Jno. 3. 3, 12; 1. 12, 13. Gal. 3. 26. Eph. 1. 4, 5. Tit. 3. 5. Jas. 1. 18. 1 Pet. 1. 23. 1 Jno. 3. 1, 2; 2. 29.
Its effect—1 Jno. 3. 9. Ro. 8. 14, 16, 17. Gal. 4. 6, 7; 5. 16, 25. 2 Co. 5. 17.

RESURRECTION.

Hos. 13. 14. Isa. 25. 8; 26. 19. Dan. 12. 1, 2. Job 19. 25–27. Ps. 49. 15. Acts 13. 32–37; 24. 14, 15. 1 Co. 15. 12, 13, 20, 21. Jno. 11. 25; 6. 39, 40, 44, 54. 1 Co. 15. 14, 17, 19. Jno. 14. 19. 1 Co. 15. 35–38. Lu. 20. 35–38. 1 Co. 15. 51, 52. Rev. 20. 5, 6. 1 Thess. 4. 14–17. Rev. 20. 11–13. Jno. 5. 28, 29. Matt. 25. 31, 32.
Warning—2 Tim. 2. 17, 18.

RIGHTEOUSNESS.

Of man—Isa. 64: 6. Lu. 18. 9, 10. Phi 3. 6–9.

THE BIBLE AND THE SUNDAY SCHOOL.

Of God—1 Co. 1. 30.   Ro. 1. 16, 17.   2 Co. 5. 21.   Ro. 5. 19 ;   3. 21, 22, 25, 26 ;   4. 5, 6.
A gift—Ro. 5. 17.   Tit. 3. 4, 5.
Exhortation—Eph. 4. 17, 24 ; 6. 14.
Warnings—2 Pet. 2. 20, 21.   1 Jno. 3. 7, 10.
Examples—Ro. 4. 2, 3, 19, 22.   Heb. 11. 7, 11, 32, 33.

SABBATH.

Before the Law—Ex. 16. 25, 26.
The Law Given—Ex. 20. 2, 8-11.
Its strictness—Ex. 34. 21 ; 35. 2, 3.
Reasons - Ex. 20. 11.   Deut. 5. 15.   Eze. 20. 12.   Ex. 31. 17.
Sabbath breaking—Ex. 31. 15, 16.   Num. 15. 32, 35, 36.
Sabbatic years—Lev. 25. 2, 4.   Ex. 23. 10, 11.   Neh. 10. 31.   Lev. 25. 8, 11.
Christ the Lord of the Sabbath—Mar. 2. 27, 28.   Matt. 11. 28, 29.

SALVATION.

Ro. 1. 16.   Acts 4. 10-12 ; 28. 25-28.   Ro. 10. 9, 10.   2 Pet. 3. 15.
Is of God—Phil. 2. 12, 13.   1 Thess. 5. 9.   2 Thess. 2. 13, 14.   Heb. 5. 9.   Rev. 7. 9, 10.

SANCTIFICATION.

Heb. 2. 11.   1 Co. 1. 30.   1 Tim. 4. 4, 5.   Heb. 10. 9, 10, 14.   Eph. 5. 25, 26.   Heb. 10. 29.   2 Thess. 2. 13.   Heb. 13. 12.
Exhortation—1 Thess. 4. 1-4.

SCRIPTURE, HOLY.

Inspired—2 Tim. 3. 16, 17.   2 Pet. 1. 20, 21.   1 Thess. 2. 13.   Ro. 15. 4.   1 Co. 10. 11 : 9. 9, 10.   Eph. 6. 17.
Sufficient—Lu. 16. 30.   Deut. 4. 2.   Pro. 30. 5, 6.   Rev. 22. 18, 19.
Its Power—Jno. 15. 3.   Eph. 5. 25, 26.   Jno. 17. 17.
How to be used—Neh. 8. 8.   2 Chr. 17. 9.   1 Pet. 4. 11.   Acts 18. 28.   2 Co. 2. 17, (marg.)
Testimony of Christ—Jno. 5. 39.   Lu. 24. 27.   Rev. 19. 10.   Acts 10. 43.
Divinely Taught—Lu. 24. 45.   Jno. 6. 63.   2 Co. 3. 5, 6.   Heb. 4. 12.
Ignorance of—Matt. 22. 29.   Jno. 20. 9.   Isa. 8. 20.
Our duty towards—Neh. 9. 2, 3.   Acts 17. 11, 12.   Deut. 6. 6, 7.   Jos. 1. 8.   Ps. 1. 2.   1 Pet. 2. 2, 3.   Col. 3. 16.

SIN.

Ro. 14. 23.   Job 25. 4 : 14. 4.   Ps. 51. 5.   Jer. 17. 9.   Pro. 20. 9.   Mar. 7. 21-23.

Repentance—1 Jno. 1. 9.   Jer. 3. 13.   Lu. 15. 18, 19.   Jas. 5. 16.
The remedy—Ro. 5. 6.   2 Co. 5. 21.   Heb. 4. 15.   1 Jno. 3. 5.   Jno. 1. 29.   1 Tim. 1. 15.   1 Jno. 1. 7.   Eph. 1. 7.
In believers—1 Jno. 1. 8-10.   Ro. 7. 23.   Gal. 5. 17.
How to deal with sinners—Eph. 4. 26, 32.   Gal. 6. 1.   2 Co. 2. 7, 8.   Lu. 17. 3, 4.   Matt. 18. 35.
The new birth—1 Jno. 3. 9 ; 5. 1.
Warning—Gal. 5. 19-21.

SONSHIP.

Jno. 1. 12. 13.   Ro. 8. 14-17.   Gal. 4. 4-7.   Heb. 2. 11.   1 Jno. 3. 1, 2.   Eph. 1. 4, 5.   1 Jno. 3. 9, 10.

TRIAL.

Common to all—Job 5. 7.   1 Co. 10. 13.   Jno. 16. 33.   Acts 14. 22.
Cause of rejoicing—1 Pet. 4. 12-14.   Jas. 1. 2.   Acts 5. 41.   Matt. 5. 11, 12.   Ro. 5. 3.   2 Co. 12. 9, 10.   Jno. 15. 19.   2 Co. 7. 4.   Heb. 10. 32-34.   2 Co. 4. 17.   Ro. 8. 18.   1 Pet. 1. 6.   2 Co. 1. 3-7.
Warning—Matt. 13. 20, 21.

TYPES.

Lu. 24. 27, 44.
Of dispensation—Genesis.   Gal. 4. 21-29   Heb. 7. 4, 5, 11, 24, 25.   Ps. 110. 4.
Of Redemption—Exodus.   1 Co. 5. 7.   Heb. 9. 22.
Of access to God—Leviticus, chaps. 1. 2. 3.   Heb. 9. 13, 14.   Eph. 5. 2.   Heb. 10. 8, 9.
Of experience—Numbers.   1 Co. 10. 1-11.   Acts 15. 10.
Of experience matured—Joshua.   Eph. 6. 12.   Col. 3. 3, 1.
Adam—Ro. 5. 14.   1 Co. 15. 45.
Abel—Gen. 4. 8, 10.   Acts 2. 23.   Heb. 12. 24.
Melchisedec—Heb. 7. 14, 15, 17 : 5. 10, 11.
Abraham—Gen. 17. 5.   Eph. 3. 14, 15.
Isaac—Heb. 11. 17, 19.
Moses—Acts 3. 20, 22.   Heb. 3. 5, 6.
Aaron—Heb. 5. 4, 5 ; 9. 24-26 ; 10. 21, 22.
Joshua—Heb. 4. 8, 9.
David—Eze. 37. 24.
Solomon—Lu. 1. 32, 33 : 11. 31.
Jonah—Matt. 12. 40.
Brazen Serpent—Jno. 3. 14.
Brazen Altar (Christ's sacrifice)—Ex. chap. 27.
Golden Altar (Christ's intercession)—Ex. chap. 30.
The veil—Heb. 10. 19, 20.   Jno. 10. 1, 7.
The Paschal Lamb—Jno. 1. 29 : 19. 33, 36
Manna—Jno. 6. 32, 33, 35.   1 Co. 10. 3.
The Smitten Rock—1 Co. 10. 4.

The Scape-goat—Lev. 16. 21, 22. Isa. 53. 11, 12. 1 Pet. 2. 24.

UNBELIEF.

Jno. 16. 9. Ro. 14. 23; 11. 30, 31.
Warnings—Heb. 3. 18, 19. Jno. 8. 24; 3. 18, 36. Mar. 16. 16.

WATCHFULNESS.

Matt. 13. 25-27; 24. 42, 44; 25. 5, 6, 13. Rev. 16. 15. Heb. 9. 28. Tit. 2. 12, 13. 1 Thess. 5. 6. 2 Tim. 4. 8. 2 Pet. 3. 11-13. 1 Pet. 5. 8.

WORKS.

Jno. 6. 28, 29. Ro. 11. 6. Isa. 64. 6. Gal. 2. 21. Jas. 2. 10, 20. Ro. 4. 2-5.

---

9. Bible Readings in their Various Uses.

(1.) BIBLE READINGS IN THE PRAYER MEETING OR PULPIT.

Grace.

No. 1. Its source.
    John i. 14–17; Rom. v. 15; 1 Cor. i. 3, 4.
2. All grace comes from God.
    1 Peter v. 10.
3. To whom does He offer grace
    Matt. xxi. 31; Hosea xiii. 9; John viii. 4–12.
4. Not of works.
    Eph. ii. 8, 9; 2 Tim. i. 9; Rom. xi. 6.
5. It bringeth salvation.
    Titus ii. 11–14.
6. We are justified freely by His grace.
    Titus iii. 7; Rom. iii. 24.
7. Sin reigned unto death, but grace unto life eternal.
    Rom. v. 20, 21; vi. 1, 2.
8. We are not under law, but under grace.
    Rom. vi. 14, 15.
9. The difference between the law and grace.
    Deut. xxi. 18; Luke xv. 12–24.
10. How are we to get it?
    Heb. iv. 16.
11. His grace sufficient at all times.
    2 Cor. ix. 8; xii. 9
12. Who have it more freely?
    Eph. vi. 24; James iv. 6

13. We are to sing with grace in our hearts
   Col. v. 16.
14. What is falling from grace ?
   Gal. v. 1–5.
15 Difference between government and grace.
   (No texts ; but retributive dealings with Lot, Jacob, David, brought out, as contrasted with the Prodigal Son, and the surpassing love revealed in the Gospel.)
16. Last words of Peter and John.
   2 Peter iii. 18 ; Rev. xxii. 21.

D L. Moody.

(2.) AT FAMILY PRAYERS

Subject, Growth in Grace. Passages to be read with brief comment :—Prov. iv. 18 ; Eph. iv. 14, 15 ; Psa. lxxxiv. 5, 7 ; 1 Cor. iii. 18 ; 2 Pet. iii. 18 ; Phil. iii. 12, 14.

H. B. Chamberlin.

(3.) BIBLE READING ON THE LESSON IN THE TEACHERS' MEETING.

The Good Shepherd. John x. 11-18.

1. BIBLE SHEPHERDS. Gen. lxvii. 3 ; Exod. ii. 17 ; Luke ii. 8, 20 ; 1 Sam. xvi. 11, 19 ; Matt. xv. 24.
2. THE LORD MY SHEPHERD. Psa. xxiii. 1, 4 ; 1 Pet. ii. 25 ; v. 4 ; Heb. xiii. 20, 21.
3. HE KNOWS HIS SHEEP. John x. 14 ; Ezek. xxxv. 11, 13 ; 2 Tim. ii. 19 ; John x. 27.
4. HE PROVIDES FOR HIS SHEEP. John x. 9 ; Psa. xviii. 1, 2 ; Isa. lxv. 11 ; Psa. xxxiv. 10 ; Rom. viii. 28.
5. HE GUIDES HIS SHEEP. John x. 3, 16 ; Psa. xxiii. 3 ; Prov. viii. 28 ; Psa. xlviii. 14 ; John xvi. 13.
6. HE GIVES HIS LIFE FOR HIS SHEEP. John xviii. 11, 15 ; Isa. liii. 6 ; Rom. v. 8 ; Eph. v. 2 ; Tit. ii. 14.
7. HE DELIGHTS IN HIS SHEEP. John x. 28-30 ; Mal. iii. 17 ; 1 Pet. ii. 9 ; Rev. vii. 17 ; Psa. ciii. 13.

J. H. Vincent, D.D.

(4.) BIBLE READING AS A REVIEW OF THE LESSON

RESPONSIVE READING, with Bible Readings.*

[From "Historic Hymns," a Praise Circular, published by D. Lothrop & Co., Boston, consisting of Scripture and Hymns for Religious Meetings.]

[Luke xv. 2, etc.]

Leader.—And he said, A certain man had two sons.

Congregation.—And the younger of them said to his father, Father, give me the portion of goods that falleth to me. And he divided unto them his living.

L.—And not many days after the younger son gathered all together, and took his journey into a far country, and there wasted his substance with riotous living.

  No. 1. Isa. liii. 6.* No. 2. Isa. i. 5, 6.
    No. 3. Rom. iii. 23.

L.—And when he had spent all, there arose a mighty famine in that land; and he began to be in want.

  No. 4. Rom. vii. 24. No. 5. Isa. lvii. 20, 21.

L.—And he went and joined himself to a citizen of that country; and he sent him into his fields to feed swine.

C.—And he would fain have filled his belly with the husks that the swine did eat; and no man gave unto him.

  No. 6. Isa. lv. 1, 2. No. 7. Psa. l. 15.

(Sing, "Prodigal child, come home, come home.")

L.—And when he came to himself, he said, How many hired

---

* These passages for Bible reading should be indicated on slips of paper, and handed before the meeting to various parties, who will either repeat them or read them from Bibles when called for. It will save much time and explanations to have a supply of blanks printed as follows :—

    No..................

Please look out this passage of Scripture, and be ready to read it when called for by number. Book of.. ....chapter.......................

servants of my father have bread and to spare, and I perish with hunger.

(Sing, " Arise, my soul, arise.")

L.—I will arise and go to my father, and will say unto him, Father, I have sinned against heaven, and before thee.

C.—And am no more worthy to be called thy son ; make me as one of thy hired servants.

    No. 8. Psa. li. 4.   No. 9. Luke xviii. 13.

L.—And he arose and came to his father. But when he was yet a great way off, his father saw him, and had compassion, and ran, and fell on his neck, and kissed him.

    No. 10. Heb. x. 22.   No. 11. Matt. xi. 28.

L.—And the son said unto him, Father, I have sinned against heaven, and in thy sight, and am no more worthy to be called thy son.

    No. 12. Psa. xli. 3.

L.—But the father said to his servants, Bring forth the best robe, and put it on him ; and put a ring on his hand, and shoes on his feet.

C.—And bring hither the fatted calf, and kill it; and let us eat and be merry.

L.—For this my son was dead, and is alive again ; he was lost, and is found. And they began to be merry.

(Sing, " Ring the bells of heaven.")

    No. 13. 1 John i. 9.   No. 14. Luke xv. 7.
    No. 15. John xiv. 2, 3.   No. 16. 2 Cor. v. 1.
           No. 17. Psa. xvi. 11.

W. F. Crafts.

(5.) BIBLE READINGS IN STUDYING BIBLE BOOKS.

THE FOUR GOSPELS.

By Rev. A. H. Munro.

It is a remarkable fact that there are *only* four accepted

gospels when so many pretended ones were written, and that there are as many as four recognised by the whole church as genuine and authentic. The Divine Spirit guided in the selection as well as in the composition of the gospels.

1. Many comparisons have been made in relation to them. Irenæus compared them to the four quarters of the globe, to four columns, four winds; Augustine, to four trumpets; Calvin, to four horses drawing Christ's chariot. The best of such comparisons, because an aid to memory, is that of the cherubic symbol in Ezekiel i. 10; or, what is preferable, in the order given in Rev. iv. 7, of the symbolic forms of the lion, ox, man, and eagle, the coincidences recalling the special nature of each gospel.

Matthew's emblem is the lion. In his gospel, Christ is presented as the lion of the tribe of Judah; the root of David; the Shiloh; the King of the Jews; "the son of David;" the son of Abraham.—Matt. i. 1.

Mark's emblem is the ox, the oriental symbol of patient toil. In his gospel Christ is the Son of God, in his humiliation making himself of no reputation; the divine servant and worker.

Luke's emblem is the face of man. Christ is traced to Adam, not to David or Abraham; the Son of man in his humanity as the teacher and healer of ours.

John's emblem is the eagle. In his gospel we are carried to the sublimest heights, and behold Christ descending from heaven, not the Son of David, Abraham or Adam, but of God.

2. *Authorship.*

That Matthew's gospel was written by the disciple whose name it bears is proved (1) by the name; (2) by tradition; (3) by coincidences between the man and the book.

Notice the variation in the accounts of his call as given in Matt. ix. 9; Mark ii. 14; Luke v. 27, 28. As illustrating his Christian modesty, Matthew omits to mention that he was Levi, the son of Alpheus, and that he left all and made a great feast for Jesus. But he mentions what the others omit—

that he was a publican. His modesty is also exhibited by the difference in the order of the disciples' names in Matt. ii. 4; Mark iii. 16, 19; Luke vi. 13, 16; in his record of the disrepute in which publicans were held—Matt. v. 46, 47; ix. 11; xi. 19; xviii. 17; xxi. 31; and also in his omission of all favourable to publicans, as the conversion of Zaccheus, Luke xix. 2; the parable of the Pharisee and publican.

His business habits caused his gospel to be more systematic than the others. He groups things of the same kind—discourses, parables, miracles. As discourses, in Matt. v. to vii.; parables in chap. xiii.; and miracles in chaps. viii. and ix.

Mark was the John Mark mentioned in Acts xii. 12, 25; xiii. 5, 13; xv. 39; Col. iv. 10; 1 Pet. v. 13. Supposed by some to be the young man mentioned in Mark xiv. 51, 52. Referred to by Paul, Phil. xxiv. 2; Tim. iv. 11.

According to tradition this gospel is Peter's, Mark being only his amanuensis. Internal evidences: For instance, he mentions things he would be likely to know or observe—see Mark i. 29; Luke iv. 38; Matt. xxi. 20; and Mark xi. 13, 14, 21. He omits anything that specially honoured Peter: his walking on the sea, Matt. xiv. 28, 31; also Matt. xvi. 13, 19; xix. 28; John xxi. 15, 19; and that he was the first of the disciples to whom Jesus appeared. Inserts all discreditable to himself, as Mark viii. 32, 33; compare Matt. xxvi. 75, and Mark xiv. 72; but mentions the message sent specially to him, Mark xvi. 7.

LUKE.

Little known of him. Said to be one of the 70, but this is not probable, Luke i. 2. Tradition and Luke i. and Acts i. proofs of his authorship. A Gentile convert, Col. iv. 11; a physician, Col. iv. 14; Paul's companion, Acts xvi. 11, and 2 Tim. iv. 11. Effects of his education: His gospel more strictly historical; it and Acts alone have dedications. His history, complete, begins earlier, ends later; gives particulars about the Saviour's youth; has more references to dates and coeval events, &c. See Luke i. 5; ii. 1, 2; iii. 1; ii. 21; ii. 33; ii. 37; iii. 42; ix. 20; ix. 28; xiii. 16. Traces of his profession; quotation of Isa. lxi. 1; in Luke iv. 18; also in Luke iv. 23. Compare Matt. viii. 14 and Luke iv. 38; Matt. viii. 15, Luke

iv. 39, Matt. viii. 2, and Luke v. 12 ; Matt. viii. 6, and Luke vii. 2 ; Matt. ix. 20, and Luke viii. 43. Influence of Paul ; Compare Luke xxii. 17, 20 and 1st Cor. xi. 23, 26. Predilection for triplets, 1 Cor. xiii. 13 ; 1 Thes. v. 23 ; 2 Cor. xiii. 13. Matthew gives the parable of the lost sheep, Luke adds those of the lost piece of silver and the prodigal son. See also Matt. vii. 9, 10, and Luke xi. 11, 12 ; Matt. xxiv. 40 ; Luke xvii. 34, 36 ; Matt. viii. 19, 22 ; and Luke ix. 57, 62.

John.

Tradition says he wrote this gospel to present an aspect of Christ's nature apt to be too little regarded by readers of the other gospels—the divinity of Christ. John was not what the painters have represented him, an effeminate man, but with much of force and fire in his nature, yet a reverent, loving man, with special gifts of insight. These points are illustrated by his never giving the name of John to any one but the Baptist. His delineation of his character in John iii. 25, 36 ; also in his record of the mingled familiarity and reverence marking the intercourse between Christ and his disciples—John iv. 27 ; xiii. 23, 36. His love is shown in Mary being committed to his care ; in his full account of Peter's restoration—John xxi. 15, 19 ; and in his making a companion of Peter—John xxi. 7 ; Acts iii. 1.

His gospel was written after the destruction of Jerusalem ; see John xi. 18, and xviii. 1—hence safe to relate the resurrection of Lazarus—and John xviii. 10, and xviii 26, which compare with xviii. 16.

3. *Peculiarities of Style in the Four Gospels.*

In Matthew, " Then " occurs 90 times (in Mark vi. and Luke xiv.) ; Kingdom of heaven, 33 times ; Heavenly Father, 6 times ; Father in Heaven, 16 times ; Church, twice.

In Mark, " straightway " or " immediately " occurs 41 times. Vividness of description, as in Mark i. 13 ; i. 33. Compare Matt. ix. 2 ; Mark ii. 3, 4 ; Matt. viii. 23, 25, and Mark iv. 36, 38.

Luke's favorite expression, used also by Matthew, and less frequently by Mark, is "And it came to pass."

John's favorite expression is "After," and "After these things," and "light," and "life."

4. *The classes to whom they were specially addressed.*

Matthew wrote especially for Jews in Palestine; hence he gives no explanation of Jewish customs or topography, and shows the fulfilment of the Old Testament in the New.

Mark wrote for Gentile converts in Palestine, like Cornelius; hence Jewish customs are explained, but a knowledge of the country assumed.

Luke wrote for Gentiles everywhere; hence Christ is traced to Adam, Jewish customs and chronology made intelligible to a foreigner, and the parables of the Good Samaritan and Prodigal Son introduced.

John's Gospel was written for mankind. In it Christ is the light of the world, and in it no knowledge of Jewish custom or topography is assumed.

5. *Subject matter of the four Gospels.*

Matthew.—The gospel of the discourses and miracles—of types and fulfilment of prophecy. Christ, the true Israel, called out of Egypt, true Solomon to whom the East brings its treasures, the true Moses who gives the law; the wonder-worker, teacher, high priest. Gospel of warning. Prophetic warning, Matthew xxiv. and xxv. The high priest rends his clothes, Matthew xxvi. 65, and God rends the veil of the temple, Matthew xxvii. 51. Pilate's wife dreams, and Pilate washes hands, and the people imprecate on themselves the blood of Him whom the Gentile centurion confessed to be the Son of God. Matthew xxvii. 19, 24, 25, 54.

Mark is the gospel of action. Christ is here the mighty worker. Rabbi, not Lord (only so addressed by the Syro-Phœnician woman).

There are but few parables in this gospel. Instances, Mark iv. 1, 19; iv. 14, 20; iv. 26, 29; iv. 13, 30, 32; xii. 1, 12; xiii. 28, 29; xiii. 34, 37.

Personal traits of Christ are recorded in this gospel, not found elsewhere, as in Mark xi. 11, and x. 32; and also mention in several places of Christ's being moved, grieved, loving, sighing. Only in Mark do we find the words in Mark ii. 27 and iv. 39.

Luke.—Christ's humanity more fully delineated as babe, child, lad, man. Only in this gospel do we read of Christ's eating earthly food after his resurrection—Luke xxiv. 30, 43. Compare John ii. 13, 15. His human sympathies more fully set forth. For children. Infants brought to him. The only daughter of Jairus, and only son of the father who besought him. For women, Mary and Elisabeth, and Anna, Martha and Mary, the women that ministered to him, viii. 2, 3. The daughters of Jerusalem, xxiii. 28. For widows, iv. 25; xx. 47; ii. 37; vii. 12; xviii. 3, 5; xxi 2, 3. For the poor and outcasts. Illustrated by the parable of the rich man and Lazarus, Zaccheus, the woman who was a sinner, and the parables in Luke xv.

John's Gospel is remarkable for peculiar terms applied to Christ: The Word, Only begotten, Life, Light, Lamb,—all designed to set Him forth as the Divine Saviour of men.

He alone of the evangelists indulges in comment, as John vii. 39; xi. 51; xi. 13.

He omits parables, with the partial exceptions of John x. 1, 16, and xv. 1, 5; because he does not record Christ's popular discourses, but His private conversations with His disciples, and theological discussions with the highly educated Pharisees and Sadducees.

He repeats only two of the miracles recorded by the other evangelists—the feeding of the five thousand, and the walking on the sea. The explanation of the first of these, in John vi. 35, 51, makes known to us that miracles are parables, and form a complete system illustrated by the miracles of resurrection, of which the first was that of an only daughter, the second that of an only son, the third that of an only brother. The first, that of one just dead; the second dead one being carried to the grave; the third, that of one buried four days. The culminating miracle of resurrection is that of Him who was the only begotten Son of God.

The divinity of John the Voice V. 23. JOHN, I. *John the Baptist's testimony of Christ.*

6 ¶ There was a man, sent from God, whose name was John.
7 The same came for a witness, to bear witness of the Light, that all men through him might believe.
8 He was not that Light, but was sent to bear witness of that Light.
9 That was the true Light, which lighteth every man that cometh into the world.
10 He was in the world, and the world was made by him, and the world knew him not.
11 He came unto his own, and his own received him not.
12 But as many as received him, to them gave he power to become the sons of God, even to them that believe on his name:
13 Which were born, not of blood, nor of the will of the flesh, nor of the will of man, but of God.
14 And the Word was made flesh, and dwelt among us, (and we beheld his glory, the glory as of the only begotten of the Father,) full of grace and truth.
15 ¶ John bare witness of him, and cried, saying, This was he of

CHAP. 1.
e Malachi 3, 1.
f Acts 13, 25.
g Isaiah 49, 6.
1 John 2, 8.
h Psalm 33, 6.
1 Cor. 8, 6.
Eph. 3, 9.
Col. 1, 17.
i Heb. 1, 2.
Heb. 11, 3.
Rev. 4, 11.
k Luke 19, 14.
l Isaiah 56, 5.
Romans 8, 15.
Gal. 3, 26.
2 Peter 1, 4.
1 John 3, 1.
1 Or, the right, or, privilege.
h Deut. 30, 6.
chap. 3, 5.
James 1, 18.
1 Peter 1, 23.
l Matth. 1, 20.
1 Tim. 3, 16.
1 John 1, 1.
m Romans 1, 3.
n Heb. 2, 14.
z Isaiah 40, 5.
Matth. 17,

25 And they asked him, and said unto him, Why baptizest thou then, if thou be not that Christ, nor Elias, neither that prophet?
26 John answered them, saying, I baptize with water: but there standeth one among you, whom ye know not;
27 He it is, who coming after me, is preferred before me, whose shoe's latchet I am not worthy to unloose.
28 These things were done in Bethabara beyond Jordan, where John was baptizing.
29 ¶ The next day John seeth Jesus coming unto him, and saith, Behold the Lamb of God, which taketh away the sin of the world! 1 Jno. 2, 2.
30 This is he of whom I said, After me cometh a man which is preferred before me: for he was before me.
31 And I knew him not: but that he should be made manifest to Israel, therefore am I come baptizing with water.
32 And John bare record, saying, I saw the Spirit descending from

we received, and grace for grace. 17 For the Law was given by Moses, *but* grace and truth came by Jesus Christ. 18 No man hath seen God at any time; the only begotten Son, which is in the bosom of the Father, he hath declared *him*.

19 ¶ And this is the record of John, when the Jews sent priests and Levites from Jerusalem to ask him, Who art thou?

20 And he confessed, and denied not; but confessed, I am not the Christ.

21 And they asked him, What then? Art thou Elias? And he saith, I am not. Art thou that prophet? And he answered, No.

22 Then said they unto him, Who art thou? that we may give an answer to them that sent us. What sayest thou of thyself?

23 He said, I *am* the voice of one crying in the wilderness, Make straight the way of the Lord, as said the prophet Esaias.

24 And they which were sent were of the Pharisees.

25 [continued] water, the same said unto me, Upon whom thou shalt see the Spirit descending, and remaining on him, the same is he which baptizeth with the Holy Ghost.

34 And I saw and bare record that this is the Son of God.

35 ¶ Again, the next day after, John stood, and two of his disciples;

36 And looking upon Jesus as he walked, he saith, Behold the Lamb of God!

37 And the two disciples heard him speak, and they followed Jesus.

38 Then Jesus turned, and saw them following, and saith unto them, What seek ye? They said unto him, Rabbi, (which is to say, being interpreted, Master,) where dwellest thou?

39 He saith unto them, Come and see. They came and saw where he dwelt, and abode with him that day: for it was about the tenth hour.

40 One of the two which heard John speak, and followed him, was Andrew, Simon Peter's brother.

Col. 2, 9.
Exodus 20, 1.
Rom. 3, 21.
chap. 14, 6.
Exod. 33, 20.
1 John 4, 9.
Prov. 8, 30.
Malachi 4, 5.
Luke 1, 17.
Isaiah 40, 3.
Malachi 3, 1.
Exodus 12, 3.
Isaiah 53, 7.
1 Peter 1, 19.
Rev. 6, 6.
1 Cor. 15, 3.
Gal. 1, 4.
Heb. 1.
Heb. 2, 17.
Heb. 9, 28.
1 John 2, 2.
Rev. 1, 5.
Or, beareth.
Acts 2, 4.
Or, abidest.
That was two hours before night.

15 Titles of Christ in ch. 1.
V. 1. Word. *God.* *V. 5. The Life.*
Jesus The Word V. 17
John the Voice V. 23
The divinity of the Word. JOHN, I. *John the Baptist's testimony of Christ.*

CHAP. 1.
a Malachi 3, 1.
f Acts 13, 25.
g Isaiah 49, 6.
1 John 2, 8.
h Psalm 33, 6.
1 Cor. 8, 6.
Eph. 3, 9.
Col. 1, 17.
Heb. 1, 2.
Heb. 11, 3.
Rev. 4, 11.
i Luke 19, 14.
j Isaiah 54, 5.
Romans 8, 15.
Gal. 3, 26.
1 Peter 1, 4.
1 John 3, 1.
3 Or, the right, or, privilege.
k Deut. 29, 6.
chap. 3, 5.
James 1, 18.
1 Peter 1, 23.
l Matth. 1, 20.
1 Tim. 3, 16.
1 John 1, 1.
m Romans 1, 3.
n Heb. 2, 16.
o Isaiah 40, 5.
Matth. 17, 2.
2 Peter 1, 17.
p Col. 2, 3.
q Col. 1, 17.
r Eph. 7, 6.
Col. 2, 9.
s Exodus 20, 1.
t Rom. 3, 21.
u chap. 14, 6.
v Exod. 33, 20.
w 1 John 4, 9.
x Prov. 8, 30.
y Malachi 4, 5.
z Luke 1, 17.
2 *Or,* ———
a Isaiah 40, 3.
b Malachi 3, 1.
c Exodus 12, 3.
Isaiah 53, 7.
1 Peter 1, 19.
Rev. 5, 6.
d 1 Cor. 15, 3.
Gal. 1, 4.
Heb. 1, 3.
Heb. 2, 17.
Heb. 9, 28.
1 John 2, 2.
Rev. 1, 5.
e Or, *breaketh.*
f Acts 2, 4.
4 Or, *abideth.*
5 That was two hours before night.

6 ¶ There *b* was a man sent from God, whose name was John.
7 The same came for a witness, to bear witness of *the Light,* that all *men* through him might believe.
8 He *c* was not that Light, but *was sent* to bear witness of that Light.
9 *That d* was the true Light, which lighteth every man that cometh into the world.
10 He was in the world, and *e* the world was made by him, and the world knew him not.
11 He *f* came unto his own, and his own received him not.
12 But *g* as many as received him, to them gave he *³ power* to become the *sons of God, even* to them that believe on his name:
13 Which *h* were born, not of blood, nor of the will of the flesh, nor of the will of man, *but of God.*
14 And *i* the Word *m* was made *n* flesh, and dwelt among us, (and we *o* beheld his glory, the glory as of the only begotten of the Father,) full *p* of grace and truth.
15 ¶ John bare witness of him, and cried, saying, This was he of whom I spake, He that cometh after me is preferred before me: for *q* he was before me.
16 And of his *r* fulness have all we received, and grace for grace.
17 For the *s* Law was given by Moses, *t but grace and u truth* came by *Jesus Christ.*
18 No *v* man hath seen God at any time; the *w* only begotten Son, which is in *x* the bosom of the Father, he hath declared him.
19 ¶ And this is the record of John, when the Jews sent priests and Levites from Jerusalem to ask him, Who art thou?
20 And he confessed, and denied not; but confessed, I am not the Christ.
21 And they asked him, What then? Art thou *y* Elias? And he saith, *z* I am not. Art thou *²* that prophet? And he answered, No.
22 Then said they unto him, Who art thou? that we may give an answer to them that sent us. What sayest thou of thyself?
23 He said, I *am* the voice of one crying in the wilderness, Make straight the way of the Lord, as said *a* the prophet Esaias.
24 And they which were sent were of the Pharisees.

25 And they asked him, and said unto him, Why baptizest thou then, if thou be not that Christ, nor Elias, neither that prophet?
26 John answered them, saying, I baptize with water: *b* but there standeth one among you, whom ye know not;
27 He it is, who coming after me, is preferred before me, whose shoe's latchet I am not worthy to unloose.
28 These things were done in Bethabara beyond Jordan, where John was baptizing.
29 ¶ The next day John seeth Jesus coming unto him, and saith, Behold *c* the Lamb of God, *d* which *e* taketh away the sin of the world.
30 This is he of whom I said, After me cometh a man which is preferred before me: for he was before me. *taketh place*
31 And I knew him not: but that he should be made manifest to Israel, therefore am I come baptizing with water.
32 And John bare record, saying, I saw the Spirit descending from heaven like a dove, and it abode upon him.
33 And I knew him not: but he that sent me to baptize with water, the same said unto me, Upon whom thou shalt see the Spirit descending and remaining on him, the *same is he which* baptizeth with the Holy Ghost.
34 And I saw and bare record that this is the Son of God.
35 ¶ Again, the next day after, John stood, and two of his disciples;
36 And looking upon Jesus as he walked, he saith, Behold the Lamb of God!
37 And the two disciples heard him speak, and they followed Jesus.
38 Then Jesus turned, and saw them following, and saith unto them, What seek ye? They said unto him, Rabbi, (which is to say, being interpreted, Master,) where *dwellest thou?*
39 He saith unto them, Come and see. They came and saw where he dwelt, and abode with him that day: for it was *about* the tenth hour.
40 One of the two which heard John speak, and followed him, was Andrew, Simon Peter's brother.

10.—BIBLE MARKING

(From " The Illustrated Christian Weekly," of the American Tract Society, New York.)

What is the best Commentary on the Bible?

The one you make yourself.

For this purpose you need a good Reference Bible, a Bible text-book, a Bible Atlas (unless yours is a Teacher's Bible, which contains all these conveniences), a Concordance, a black-lead pencil, or a good pen and ink, and—brains. It is a great mistake to suppose that the first will suffice without the last.

We will suppose that your theme for study is the first chapter of John. Your Bible lies open before you, presenting the page a fac-simile of which we give herewith from the *large print edition* of the Teacher's Bible. You believe that no prophecy is of private interpretation. You therefore begin by asking the Spirit of God to open to you the truth contained for you in this chapter. Then you read it over, at first rapidly; you aim to get a bird's-eye view of it as a whole; you see that its theme is the character, office and work of Christ. Your question then is this: What does this chapter teach me of Christ?

The first thing that strikes you is that a number of names are given to Him here. You count them: Light, Only-begotten of the Father, Jesus Christ, Only-begotten Son, the Lord, the Lamb of God, Son of God, Master, Jesus of Nazareth, the Son of Joseph, King of Israel, Son of Man. Then He is the Teacher, the Son of God, the Saviour (Jesus, Matt. i. 16), the Master, the Atoning Sacrifice, the Incarnate One, the true Man and therefore the perfect Example, the future King. You draw a heavy black line under each title: you connect them, as in the accompanying page, by a light line. You now have a body of Christology on a page of your Bible. If you have wrought this out for yourself you have done a good day's work; certainly if you have taken home to yourself the truth that he is *your* King, *your* Saviour, *your* Sacrifice, *your* Example.

The next day you return to your study again. You take up a single passage, verses 12 and 13. Who are the sons of God? As many as received him and were born of God. How? You put your references now in requisition. You look them up. You turn to your Bible Text-book under *Regeneration*. You pass by many texts that at another time will strike you, but do not now. The result of your studies is embodied in a note at the foot of the page: They are born *of* the Spirit, John iii. 15; *by* the Word of God, 1 Peter i. 2, 3; *with* the Word of truth, James i. 18; *in* Christ Jesus, 1 Cor. iv. 13; who is himself the Only-begotten Son of God, verse 18. You have here, in four verses of Scripture, the source, the instrument, the accompaniment, and the result of the new birth. You begin again: What is it to receive Christ? The result of your studies is embodied again in certain references which impress you, and which you accordingly underscore, and in certain other references which you discover, and therefore add in the margin.

But you have not exhausted this subject. You return to it on the morrow. You study the negatives. Not of blood; nor of the will of the flesh; nor of man; but of God. Your Concordance will tell you the meaning of born of blood, if your own thought has not suggested it to you; the sons of God are not brought out by merely good breeding, good parentage; Rom. viii. 3, 4, 8, 9, tell you what is the meaning of *flesh*, viz., man in his natural state; we are not born into the kingdom by our own resolution; the will of man is interpreted to you by 1 Cor. iii. 5-7; we are not brought into the kingdom of God by human endeavors. There are three theories of moral reform—good blood, strong will, good education—all repudiated; and in contrast with them the true Scripture view, the new birth by the Spirit of God, as interpreted in your verses below.

We have scarcely opened our theme; but we have done enough to give those of our readers who desire to study the Bible, and to preserve the results of their study in their Bible, some idea of how to do it.

Every student will invent, to some extent, his own system, but certain principles of universal application are inculcated by Mrs. Stephen Menzies, of England, from whose little book, "Hints on Bible Marking," we have taken some of the markings, using, however, the Teacher's Bible in the place of Bagster's, on account of its having more references.

In any given verse underline *only* the word or words required to suggest the thought.

Connect these *underlines* by the fine line, always at the end, never in the centre of the underline.

If a connection is needed with a reference to another page, carry the fine line, which she calls a *railway*, to the margin, and write the reference there.

Draw all lines with a ruler, and as lightly as possible, particularly the "Railways," with a very sharp hard black-lead pencil, or with a fine pen and India ink, or some good black ink; the latter is better.

Make your own marginal references as freely as possible, referring at *each* verse to the other.

It should be added that a good Commentary is a great help in such a study, in giving information as to the meaning of the original and other points, provided it is used as a help to study, not as a substitute for it. Mrs. Menzies uses Alford, and refers to it by the following mark *. But the reader may easily make his own system of notation to favorite writers, provided he does not have too many.

OTHER SIGNS USED IN BIBLE MARKING.

M—on the margin of Messianic references in the Old Testament.

†—in red beside passages for enquirers.

P. P—beside proved promises.

C—beside passages referring to childhood.

A red underline for all references to the atoning blood or the cross.

A blue underline for the promises.

A heavy black underline for warnings and judgments.

A date beside each text on which a sermon is preached.

11.—A Chart for the Personal Study of the Lesson.

By Rev. A. H. Munro.

PREPARATION.

I. INVESTIGATION.

1. External Particulars.
    The Book: its name, date, author, style, and important features.
2. Internal Particulars.
    1. When? Chronology and Connection.
    2. Where? Places—their peculiarities, relations, and associations.
    3. Who? Persons. Characters. Classes. Names. Titles. Positions. Histories.
    4. What? Words. Terms. Figures. Things. Actions. Incidents. Errors. Truths.
    5. Why? Causes. Motives. Designs.
    6. Whence? Things implied, inferred, suggested, produced.

II. PLANNING.

1. Decide upon the main theme of the lesson.
2. Select the truths to enforce it.
3. Select the particulars to set forth those truths.
4. Mark the points to be explained, proved, and illustrated.
5. Obtain the necessary explanations, proofs and illustrations. To do this,
    1. Live the truth.
    2. Look for illustrations, &c.
    3. Store them up in a note-book.
6. Arrange in order to interest and maintain logical connection.

TEACHING.

I. PURPOSES.

1. To inform as to Facts.

2. To convince as to Truths.
3. To persuade as to Duties.

II. METHODS.

1. By interesting; by clearness and brevity.
2. By precision, explanation, illustration, and appeal.
3. By definition, authority, effects, alternatives.

III. MEANS.

1. Questions—Their nature, definite, reasonable, to the purpose.
2. Narration—Indispensable.
3. Illustration—Of all, briefly; main points, elaborately.
4. Memorizing—Texts, main points and application.
5. Impressing—Truths and duties.
Modes—Direct, indirect, suggestive, elliptical, general and personal.
Employed—Vividly, briefly.
Kinds—Brief, extended, elaborate; appropriate, obvious, graphic and true.
How—Recitations, recapitulations, reviews.
How—By the teacher's reverence for the Bible, appreciation of truth, sympathy with Christ, dependence in the Holy Spirit, and wise and happy relations with his scholars.

---

12. ADULTS AS BIBLE STUDENTS IN THE SUNDAY SCHOOL.*

BY REV. H. M. PARSONS, D.D.

The Sabbath School service should be placed on an equal footing with the regular services of the Church, and attendance thereat by the pastor and members, equally with the young people, should be enforced. The time has arrived, when we must no longer be content with the demonstration of the truth by means of one man's preaching, but must return to the

---

* Read Deut. xxxi. 12, 13; Josh. viii. 25; 2 Chron. xxxiv. 29, 30.

method adopted by the Church during the first two centuries of its existence—that of having one service in which all present can participate, and ask and answer questions. This is necessary in order to bring Bible instruction up to the level of secular instruction. After a struggle extending over some years, I secured a change in the system followed in one of the oldest of New England churches, and the introduction of one under which there was preaching in the morning, a Bible service in the afternoon, and a church prayer and conference meeting in the evening—all the services having regard to the topic of the day. The plan proved eminently successful, and is still continued in that church, though I have removed to another charge, where a similar method is now followed.

This Bible service differs from the average Sunday Schools in the following points :—

(1.) It has **a name which includes the old as well as the young**.

(2.) It **takes the place of a Second Sermon**, thus enabling both pastor and people to attend it without neglecting other Services.

(3.) It emphasizes and **expects the attendance of adults** as much as the attendance of children.

(4.) It has the **regular presence and help of the pastor** as its advisory head, and also as the teacher of a large class of adults.

(5.) Its singing and other **exercises have regard to adults** as well as children.

(6.) It gives the commission, "go teach" equal honour with its kindred commission, "go preach."

The RESULTS of such a Service are :—

(1.) **Greater unity** between Church and Sunday School.

(2.) **Greater activity** among the adults of the church.

(3.) **Greater Spirituality** by increased study of God's Word. This Service caused an increase in the prayer meeting attendance from twenty to two hundred.

(4.) **Greater teaching efficiency**, by the increase in the numbers, age, and culture of the classes.

(5.) The preacher is enabled to **preach with more adaptation** to the real wants of his people, and a better understanding of Christian life. "He sometimes learns more from a washerwoman in his Bible Service than from his best commentaries."

---

13. ADDITIONAL HINTS ON HOW TO STUDY THE BIBLE.

AN INSTITUTE CONVERSATION.

(1.) Have for constant use a **portable Reference Bible**. (2.) **Carry** a Bible or Testament with you. (3.) Don't be afraid of **marking** it, or making notes on the margin: promises, exhortations, warnings to Christians, and invitations to the unsaved.* (4.) Do not be satisfied with simply reading a chapter, but **study the meaning** of at least one verse every day. (5.) Study so as to ascertain **the whole truth** contained in a single incident or miracle: when and why written, how it applies to yourself, and how to use it for others. (6.) Study to know **for what**, and to whom a book or chapter was written. Study the Acts of the Apostles and the Epistles **together**, also Leviticus and Hebrews, etc. (7.) BELIEVE in the Bible as **God's revelation to you**, and ACT accordingly. (8.) **Learn at least one verse of Scripture each day**. Verses from memory will be wonderfully useful in your daily life and work. See Josh. i. 8; Psa. cxix. 11. (9.) Study HOW to **use the Bible so as to "walk with God"** and lead others to Christ. (10.) Set apart at least **fifteen minutes each day for studying it**; this little will be grand in result, and never be regretted. (11.) Read the Book as if it were **written for yourself**. (12.) Always **ask God to help you** to understand it, and then EXPECT that He will.

---

*There are some in whose minds marks like these would prevent fresh thought on the marked passage, new and deeper views of its meaning. For such persons it may be best to have one Bible for marking and another for ordinary reading, the marked Bible being referred to when occasion requires, as a personal commentary.

(13.) Have **Cruden's Concordance** and a Bible Text-Book at hand; also in all cases refer to parallel passages and marginal notes, and take time to think before consulting commentaries. (14.) Study the Bible in **the freshness of the morning** rather than the weary hours of evening. (15.) Read **systematically**, with some purpose in mind. (16.) Read the Bible with a view of **living** rather than merely *learning* it, coming to it not only perfunctorily for lessons and sermons, but also **for loving conversation**, "as a man talketh with his friend."

---

14. Bill of Fare from the Bible.

Preparation.

Spread a cloth of blue, and put thereon the dishes and the spoons, and the bowls, with the bread in the basket.—Num. iv. 7, and Levit. viii. 31.

Salt without prescribing how much, and oil in a cruse.—Ezra vii. 22, and 1 Kings xvii. 12.

Tell them who are bidden I have prepared my dinner.—Matt. xxii. 4.

They are strong of appetite.—Isaiah lvi. 11.

Let us eat and be merry.—Luke xv. 23.

The feast is made for laughter.—Eccl. x. 19.

Grace.

Give us this day our daily bread.—Matt. vi. 11

God is great and God is good, And we thank him for this food:

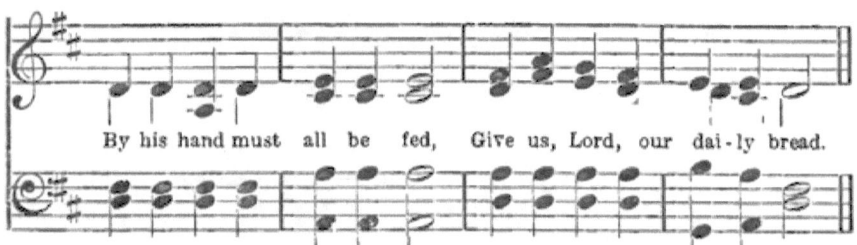

By his hand must all be fed, Give us, Lord, our dai-ly bread.

Thou openest thine hand, and satisfiest the desire of every living thing.

Soup.

Pour out the broth.—Judges vi. 20.
Feed me with pottage.—Gen. xxv. 30.
Eat this roll.—Ezek. iii. 1.

Fish.

We remember the fish we did eat freely.—Num xi. 5.
They gave him a piece of a broiled fish.—Luke xxiv. 42.
Bring of the fish which ye have now caught.—John xxi. 10.

Entremets.

Hare.—Levit. xi. 6.
Chickens.—Matt. xxiii. 37.
Besides harts and fatted fowl.—1 Kings iv. 23.

D

Relishes.

Olives.—Mic. vi. 15.
Give me a little water, for I am thirsty.—Judges iv. 19.

Roast.

All manner of baked meats.—Gen. xi. 17.
Ye may eat of the roebuck.—Deut. xii. 15.
Ye shall eat of the wild goat and wild ox.—Deut. xiv. 5.

Vegetables.

Take unto thee wheat, lentils and millet.—Ezek. iv. 9.
They brought parched corn and beans.—2 Sam. xvii. 28.
After that the full corn in the ear.—Mark iv. 28.
We remember the leeks and the onions, and the cucumbers and the garlic.—Num. xi. 5.
The manna was as coriander seed.—Num. xi. 7.

Game.

Partridges.—Jeremiah xvii. 11.
Two young pigeons.—Lev. v. 7.
And he brought quails.—Psalm cv. 40.
Carry these ten cheeses to the captain.—1 Sam. xvii. 18.

Dessert.

Behold a basket of summer fruit.—Amos viii. 1.
They brought of the pomegranates and figs.—Num xiii. 23.
Comfort me with apples.—Cant. ii. 5.
The children of Israel brought dates.—2 Chron. xxxi. 5.
Two baskets of figs.—Jeremiah xxiv. 2.
Then thou mayest eat grapes thy fill.—Deut. xxiii. 24.
We remember the melons.—Num. xi. 5.
They brought bunches of raisins.—1 Chron. xii. 40.
Carry nuts and almonds.—Gen. xiii. 11.

WHENCE COMES OUR FOOD.—Gen. i. 29 ; Psalm cxxxvi. 25 ; cvii. 9 ; cxlv. 15, 16.

HOW IT SHOULD BE EATEN.—Prov. xv. 17 ; xvii. 1 ; 1 Cor. x. 31.

SPIRITUAL FOOD.—Jer. xv. 16 ; Job. xxiii. 12 ; John vi. 32, 58 ; Isa. lv. 2 ; Matt. v. 6 ; John vi. 27.

III. THE BIBLE AND ITS TEACHERS.

An Ancient Bible School and its Teachers. Neh. viii. 1-9 ; ix. 3.

The Divine Commission to the Bible Teacher. Matt. xxviii. 19, 20 ; Jerem. i. 9 ; 2 Cor. vi. 1 ; 3 John i. 8.

Necessary Qualities of the Bible Teacher.
  (1) **Conversion.** John xxi. 15 ; 1 Sam. xvi. 7 ; John iii. 5, 10 ; 1 Sam. iii. 6 ; Acts iii. 6.
  (2) **Prayerfulness.** 1 Cor. i. 11 ; Rom. xv. 30 ; Exod. xxviii. 12, 29 ; 2 Cor. iii. 5 ; John xiv. 26.
  (3) **Consistent Example.** Acts i. 1 ; Ezra. vii. 10.
  (4) **Faithfulness and Ability to Teach.** 2 Tim. ii. 2.
  (5) **Knowledge.** 2 Pet. i. 5.
  (6) **Power of Clear Expression.** 1 Cor. xiv. 19.
  (7) **Habits of Study.** 2 Tim. ii. 15.
  (8) **Tenderness.** Psa. cxxvi. 5, 6 ; 2 Cor. ii. 4.

Summing it all up. 1 Tim. iv. 11-16.

1. Hints on the Public Use of the Bible.

AN INSTITUTE CONVERSATION.

(1) Use the Bible in every religious service, and with the utmost **honor and impressiveness**, giving the Scripture reading a place in the service where it will not be interrupted by late comers, and where all will hear it, and making it the very foundation of the exercises.

(2) In the social meetings of the Church have a pre-announced **Scripture topic** on which every one shall be expected to repeat or read a Bible passage, the reader occasionally adding words of comment and illustration.

(3) Give **great prominence** in all religious meetings to "Thus saith the Lord," showing Bible warrant for all practice and statements.

(4) **Never bang the Bible about** in the pulpit, in the Sunday School, in the prayer meeting, or in flippant conversation.

(5) **Have Bibles used by both teachers and scholars in the Sunday School** instead of the lesson leaves, which are intended for home study.*

---

* The teacher ought to bring his Bible to the class; and not the teacher alone, but the pupils too, as soon as they are able to read. *To cherish a love for God's book is the most important work a teacher has to do next to the conversion of souls.* "I do not enjoy reading my Bible; I wish I did." I have heard this remark made many times by earnest Christians. What can make the Bible more attractive? Artists are doing much to make it so, but Christian teachers can do a greater work by filling it with spiritual illuminations. These are fadeless, while the engravings endure but for a season. They can best be made from time to time when there is white heat interest in the class about the lesson by opening the Bible, and reading from it something which either confirms or continues that interest. More than likely every scholar in the class will want to read the same passages for himself during the week.

A teacher needs to speak with accuracy and authority, therefore he ought to have his Bible in his hand. Have you never seen a minister close the Bible, or lay it aside altogether before beginning to preach his sermon? or perhaps you have seen him use a rack not large enough to accommodate a Bible. As you sat and listened did you feel that you were hearing the word of God preached or the word of somebody else? At any rate you have seen a teacher conduct a class without a Bible. There is no difference in the two cases.

Bibles should be brought by the pupils to the class for three reasons at least. 1. That the teacher may know that each one owns a copy of the Bible. 2. That they may become familiar with it by learning about the relative position of its books, and how to pronounce difficult names contained in it. To many without such exercise the Bible would be a sealed book for a lifetime. 3. That habits of turning the leaves in study may be cultivated.

2. The Pastor's Relation to the Sunday School.*

Among the difficulties found in connection with this subject, are the following:—

(1.) In many cases **pastors are not consulted** in the appointment of teachers and officers.

(2.) The **non-attendance of the pastor** at Sunday School or teachers' meetings.

(3.) The failure to designate in the **constitution of the Sunday School** the pastor's relation to the school.

(4.) The assigning of **too many duties to the pastor** in connection with the church.

(5.) The **ambition of the superintendent** to rule *alone*, and his jealousy of the pastor.

(6.) **Want of greater love for Christ** and the children, in the pastor, and more spirituality on the part of the superintendent.

To meet these difficulties, the following remedies are suggested:

(1.) That a clear and correct **understanding** be established between the pastor and superintendent, as to their relative duties, at the commencement of their official connection; and that Christian **frankness** be exercised in their subsequent intercourse.

(2.) That in the constitution of every Sunday School there

The *abuse* of the lesson paper system has had a tendency to keep Bibles out of the class and out of study too. How would it do to simply indicate in the lesson papers where the passages of Scripture to be studied might be found in the Bible, that is, omitting the printing of the Scripture?
Even if this change is not made, let it be an invariable rule in a class for each person to have a Bible in his hand. The most eloquent portion of Dr. Townsend's grand speech in defence of the Bible, delivered at Chautauqua, occurred when he took up the great Bible and held it close to his heart. "And I, if I be lifted up from the earth, will draw all men unto me," is a true saying of the incarnate Word. It may be said also of the written Word.—Hon. W. F. Crafts.

* After an interesting Institute conversation on this subject it was given to a Committee of prominent Pastors and Superintendents, Rev. Richard Newton, D.D., Rev. F. H. Marling, Rev. S. L. Gracey, James Hughes, and C. M. Morton, for consideration and report. The report was as above, and was unanimously adopted by the audience of the Sunday School Parliament.

be an **explicit declaration** of the pastor's relation to the school.

(3.) That, as far as possible, the **public services** in connection with the church, **be so arranged** as to allow the pastor to devote a portion of his time to work in the Sunday School.

(4.) That **increased love for Christ** be recommended, which will lead to increased love for His lambs.

(5.) That both pastor and superintendent cultivate the spirit of Christian **charity and forbearance.**

In application of the foregoing remedies to meet the difficulties above stated, the following methods are suggested by which the pastor may aid in giving efficiency and success to the operations of the Sabbath School.

(1.) By **attending** as far as possible the teachers' meetings.

(2.) By **reviewing** the lesson.

(3.) By **preaching** to the school.

(4.) By taking part in the **selection of teachers and officers.**

(5.) By **remembering the Sunday School** in the pulpit, in prayer, preaching, and in notices.

3. Using the Bible with Enquirers

AN INSTITUTE CONVERSATION.

(1.) Have **a list of references** to passages for enquirers written **on a fly leaf of your Bible,** the passages themselves being indicated by a red cross that they may be found instantly when one has turned to the page or chapter where they are.

(2.) Use **a variety of passages** in order to reach various temperaments and experiences, representing the act of faith under the various Bible expressions, "Believe," "Receive," "Take," "Submit," etc.

(3.) Make **the promises of God**, not your experience, **the basis of the sinner's hope**, *reading* God's assurances from the open Bible, rather than merely *repeating* the passages, as a lawyer reads instead of repeating his law quotations, giving them much stronger force by so doing.

(4.) Be sure to **find out an enquirer's real intellectual and spiritual condition**, and then take the Bible passages best adapted* to his case, and apply them definitely and sympathetically.

(5.) **Urge the enquirer to get a reference Bible and Concordance** and "search the Scriptures" in order that he may become established and built up in God's truth, rather than in changeful emotions alone.

4. Passages for Enquirers used in the Moody Meetings at New York.*

Arranged by Ralph Wells.

1. I fear I shall never stand, and so dishonour Him—My circumstances are peculiar.—2 Tim. i. 12; Jude 24; Heb. xiii. 5.

2. I fear my sins are too great to be forgiven.—1 Pet. i. 18 19; Exod. xii. 13; Isa. i. 18.

3. My earthly prospects will be ruined—I shall be cast out.—Phil. iv. 19; Matt. iv. 4; Matt. xix. 29.

4. I do not feel my guilt as I should, I am waiting for conviction.—(Acts ii. 36, 38.)—Jer. xvii. 9; Prov. iii. 5; Matt. vii. 24; Zech. xii. 10.

5. I do not see that I am such a great sinner.—Isa. lxiv. 6; Rom. iii. 22, 23; 1 John i. 10.

---

* It would be an excellent practice to devote fifteen minutes at each weekly teachers' meeting to the use of the Bible with enquirers. Let the Superintendent, or Pastor, state some difficulty such as is presented by those who are seeking Christ, and ask from be teacher the appropriate passages to cancel the difficulty

6. I have made up my mind to be a Christian, but am not quite ready.—Prov. xxvii. 1 ; Matt. xxiv. 44 ; 1 Thess. v. 19 ; 2 Cor. vi. 2.

7. I will be a Christian IF———any reservation is fatal.—Luke xiv. 33 ; James iv. 4.

8. I don't know where I am—Almost distracted—Don't know whether I believe anything—What shall I do ?—John vii. 17 ; vi. 28, 29 ; Mark v. 36.

9. I do not see how to come.—Acts xiii. 39 ; Rom. x. 9 ; John iii. 36 ; Luke xv.

10. How can I know whether I am saved ?—John v. 24 ; 1 John iii. 14, 24.

11. How is it that Christ's death can avail for my sins ?—2 Cor. v. 21 ; Gal. iii. 13 ; 1 Pet. ii. 24.

12. How do I know He calls me ; am I certainly invited ? —John vi. 37 ; x. 9 ; Rev. xxii. 17.

13. How do you reconcile this, and that, in the scriptures ? —2 Cor. v. 20 ; 2 Pet. iii. 16 ; Matt. vi. 33.

14. I once loved the Lord, but have wandered far, far from Him : Is there hope for such ?—Jer. iii. 12 ; Hos. xiv. 4 ; Luke xxii. 32.

15. Why is Faith in Jesus alone enough, without any addition.—Gal. ii. 20 ; 2 Cor. v. 7 ; Rom. xi. 20 ; 1 John v. 4.

16. I have tried, and tried in vain to prepare to come to Jesus, but am as far off as ever.—Rom. x. 1-4.

---

5. "How can We get Rid of Incompetent Teachers ?"

AN INSTITUTE CONVERSATION.

1. Use more care in appointing teachers, the pastor and superintendent jointly nominating each teacher, and the officers and teachers electing or rejecting the nomination.

2. Have each teacher sign, or take publicly, some covenant of fidelity to his work.

3. Have a teachers' library in each Sunday School, and also introduce the best Sunday School periodicals.

4. Hold regular teachers' meetings, and make a teacher's continuance in his position depend upon attending it.

5. Remove existing incompetency as far as possible by more local institutes and conversations.

6. When these methods are not sufficient, let the Superintendent, by some casual remark to the teacher, show that he perceives his inefficiency.*

7. Let the teachers unite in adopting a law that two unnecessary absences of a teacher from Sunday School during a quarter, causes the forfeiture of his position.†

8. When milder measures fail let the Superintendent frankly and kindly say to the incompetent teacher that his class is dissatisfied or his work is unsatisfactory, and his resignation desired; sacrificing the feelings of one person, if need be, rather than the deepest interests of the whole class.‡

---

6. Three Requisites in Religious Teaching.

BY REV. B. P. RAYMOND.

I. An Authoritative Religious Truth.
1. The Bible.

---

* When you have an inefficient teacher, and you may know them because they always get through first, go to them and say, "Well, Miss A., I see you get through before the rest." Let her know that you notice it; ask her why she can't hold the attention of the pupils longer. She may ask you if you are going to interfere with her in that manner, and you tell her yes, and she may say perhaps she had better give up the class, and then be very careful that you don't say something to prevent her giving it up.

J. H. Vincent.

† "I ain't a comin' no more after to-day,—I ain't a-goin' to be turned over to any fellow as turns up,—I like to have a teacher as belongs to you," were the remarks of a scholar whose teacher could not stand Sunday dust, and heat, and rain, and mud half so well as on week days.

‡ In some schools the rule has been adopted by vote of the teachers and officers that scholars may change from one class to another by applying to the Superintendent. Incompetent teachers, when their classes begin to diminish rapidly, are thus led to the desired resignation without any direct action of the officers.

II. A well-defined idea of truth.
1. Intellectually.
2. Experimentally.

III. A medium to convey the truth
1. Language—Things, acts, tones, words cultivated. By
   1. Study of the Bible.
   2. Baptism of the Holy Spirit.

---

7. THE SECRET OF TEACHING WITH POWER.

BY M. C. HAZARD, ESQ.*

1. Secret of Power.

Negatively—1. Not in learning.
   2. Not in ability to talk.
   3. Not in ability merely to instruct.

Positively—1. A Christian life—on the employment of unconverted teachers—See Ps. l. 16, 17.
   2. An attractive Christian life.
   3. Tact.
   4. By attention—attention must be secured. It is compelled or attracted.

Why do pupils give attention?
1. Interest in the lesson.
2. Interest in the teacher.
3. Because other pupils do.
4. Because of the love of knowledge.
5. Because they are fed.

How secure attention?
1. By establishing the circuit of sympathy.
2. By Enthusiasm.

---

* Editor of the "National Sunday School Teacher," published at Chicago, Ill., by Adams, Blackmer & Lyon. $1 50 per year. Large reduction to Clubs.

3. By Illustration.
4. By Simple Speech.
5. By Questions
6. By Pictures—an imaginary picture gallery.

Knowledge gives power.

1. Makes a man master of the situation.
2. Gives enthusiasm.

How to obtain knowledge.

1. By continuous study.
2. By fresh study; do not depend on an old study of the lesson.

The class may be incited to self-activity by

1. Plan for future lesson.
2. Asking suggestive questions.

He only teaches with power who is taught of the Holy Spirit.

THE TEACHER'S PERSONAL AND SOCIAL STUDY OF HIS CLASS.

AN INSTITUTE CONVERSATION.

1. WHY

(1.) For the same reason that every workman should understand **his material,** every farmer his soil, every physician his patients.

(2.) To know their **needs and difficulties.**

(3.) For **adaptation.**

(4.) To understand their **characters.**

(5.) That the teacher may arouse in the scholar the **appropriate emotions** and thoughts.

(6.) To know names and **natures.**

(7.) To know their peculiar **temptations** and to counteract them.

(8.) To know their **religious education** and privileges.

(9.) To know their **likes**, dislikes, reading, amusements, associates, &c.

(10.) To know their **home surroundings** and daily life.

(11.) To know their **address** in order to call and write.

(12.) To know the **results** of our progress and work.

II. How?

(1.) By **five minute sociables** before the school opens.

(2.) By **bird parties**, grape parties, &c., for little children occasionally, at teacher's home.

(3.) **Children's hour** every week at teacher's home.

(4.) **Sewing parties** of young ladies' classes.

(5.) By **loving them** and showing the Christian virtues.

(6.) By **avoiding cant.**

(7.) By **visiting** them in their homes, schools, and stores, and requesting visits from them.

(8.) By **writing** to them.

(9.) By leading the class into **religious work.**

(10.) By **noticing them** wherever met.

(11.) By inviting them singly to **the teacher's office or home.**

(12.) By becoming **companions to them.**

(13.) By **helping them in things temporal.**

8. Normal Class Training for Teachers.

By Rev. J. L. Hurlbut

I. Great need of trained teachers.

(1.) Every reason for it that there is for trained teachers in secular schools.
(2.) The failure which results from voluntary study must be supplemented by the teacher.
(3.) Short time we have with the scholars.
(4.) The book we teach and the interests at stake.
All these reasons demand trained teachers.

II. Wherein do teachers need training?

(1.) Teachers must have character.
(2.) Teachers must have spirituality.
(3.) Teachers must know the book.
(4.) Teachers must know the methods.

III. How can this training be obtained?

(1.) Teaching will help.
(2.) Studying and reading Sunday School literature.
(3.) Attendance in Sunday School Conventions, "Assemblies" and "Parliaments."

IV. How organize a Normal class?

(1.) Get teachers together and give them a competent teacher.
(2.) Make the Teachers' Meeting a Normal class.
(3.) Unite all the teachers and superintendents in the place.

V. What a Normal class propose to do?—

Answer the following questions:
(1.) Why teach the Bible?
(2.) What shall we teach from the Bible?
(3.) How teach the Bible?

VI. Methods of conducting Normal classes.

(1.) Text-book with recitations and reviews conducted the same as in secular schools.

(2.) Leaflet method *—only a single lesson given out at a time.

(3.) Lecture method.

---

9. Qualities and Training of Primary Teachers.

BY MRS. W. F. CRAFTS.

(1.) **Age and Sex.** They may be of any sex, so that they have kept their hearts young. They may be either men or women, so they have adaptability for their work. *Mothers of little children make the best Primary Teachers.*

(2.) **A Christian.** "Lovest thou me?" was the question which Christ asked Peter before He gave him the commission "Feed my Lambs."

(3.) **An Earnest Student of the Truth.** The lesson should be kept prayerfully in the undercurrent of the teacher's thoughts all week. It requires a thorough knowledge of the lesson to be prepared to teach even the smallest children. A teacher should always know more than he attempts to teach.

(4.) **A Warm Sympathizer with Children.** A teacher who has this will observe children closely and learn their peculiar expressions, so that they may be adopted in teaching, serving as passports to the children's minds and hearts.

(5.) **Vivacity** should characterize the Primary Teacher. It should be cultivated and not assumed.

(6.) **Faith in Child Piety,** without which a Teacher could have no hope or confidence in her work, and could not work to the highest end—the conversion of the soul.

---

* Rev. J. H. Vincent, DD. 805 Broadway, N. Y., has prepared a full course of these leaflets.

(7.) A Primary Teacher's Meeting should be held for an hour each week, when the Primary Superintendent can instruct the assistants about how to teach and what to read, in order to increase intelligence and interest in the work of teaching.*

---

10. ATTENTION, DISCIPLINE, AND QUESTIONING.

BY MISS JENNY B. MERRILL.

The first step in the right direction is taken, when the teacher begins to realize that she is responsible for the attention and discipline, and that the children are not; therefore the less said to the children about it, the better. The teacher needs to study in what ways she effects the attention and discipline.

(1.) **By care for physical comfort**, that is, having regard to the ventilation, seating without crowding, frequent change of position and exercises.

(2.) **By a well-arranged programme**, prepared at home, and perfectly committed to memory, so that pauses may be avoided, which are fruitful causes of disorder. "Let the teacher not lend her efforts to keep all quiet, but to keep all employed."

(3.) **By employing the minds of children, by asking them questions.** Questions should be prepared at home. They should be asked in short well-ordered sentences, so that they will be clear and definite. They should not contain the thought that the child is expected to give in the answer, so that simple assent will be the only requirement. They should not be repeated in the same form when the children fail to understand at first, but they should be put in a more definite way. Questions should be arranged logically.

Mrs. Craft's book on methods of Primary Teaching entitled, "Open Letters to Primary Teachers," published by Nelson & Phillips, N. Y., (Price $1 00) gives the fullest discussion of questions connected with Primary and Intermedia Classes.

(4.) **By a manner evincing love, sympathy, composure, dignity, and animation.** "Fret not thyself of evil-doers." "Overcome evil with good." "A soft answer turneth away wrath." Try to inculcate right and noble views of obedience. Teach about Christ's obedience to His parents, use also Ps. xxxii. 9. Make commands requests as far as possible. Never use dictatorial tones. Do not form the habit of repeating commands before the children have time to obey, else they will form the habit of not obeying the first time. Expect to be obeyed.

11. Illustrative Teaching.[*]

by rev. w. f. crafts.

The great object of the Sunday School is not to organize its members into a pic-nic *club*, or a *library association*, or a *singing school*, or a *theological institute;* not merely to *please*, or *discipline*, or *teach*, as the *end* in view, but by *means* of all these phases of its work to accomplish its great purpose—

To present Christ

to the

Hearts of the School.

Christ is the Alpha and Omega, the beginning and the ending of Sunday School work. He must be *above all* and *in all* and *through all* the exercises.

To present Christ, then, is our object in Sunday School work. How shall we vividly and savingly present Him to the heart?

By universal consent the senses must usher truth to the soul.

---

[*] "Through the Eye to the Heart; or, Eye Teaching in the Sunday School. By Rev. W. F. Crafts. Treats of all departments of illustration. A new edition, to be ready December 1, 1876, will contain also in the Appendix blackboard exercises and other illustrations for all the international lessons of 1877. Published by Nelson & Phillips, 805 Broadway, New York. For sale by Adam Miller & Co., Toronto. Price $1.50.

The Sunday School works mainly through the two most influential senses—sight and hearing. Hearing lacks vividness without sight (the *visions* by which God taught His truth were usually more impressive than His *spoken messages*), but *sight lacks definiteness without hearing* (even the inscription in fire on Babylon's wall needed words of explanation). It is well, therefore, that hearing and seeing should accompany each other. Joseph's brethren brought to their father, who had long mourned for Joseph as dead, this wonderful message: "Thus saith thy son Joseph, I am yet alive; come down unto me, tarry not." Jacob's heart fainted when he simply *heard* these words, for he believed them not; but "when he *saw the wagons* which Joseph had sent to carry him, the spirit of Jacob their father revived." The wagons would have meant nothing unless they had been preceded by the message; the message would have failed unless it had been followed by the wagons. This shows us how to use the eye and ear in the Sunday School. Give what "is written," and then, by maps, picture objects, blackboard exercises, and stories, put it into "wagons" to help the imagination and the understanding, and send it through "eye-gate," into the soul.

I want to say at once, lest any should be prejudiced against this subject, that unless there is "*a living spirit in the wheels*" these illustrative wagons are utterly useless.

"'Tis *love* must drive the chariot wheels."

Eye-Teaching is Philosophical.

Sight seems to be connected with each of the other senses. We say of food we have been describing, "Taste and *see;*" we say of the fragrance of a flower of which we have been speaking, "Smell and *see;*" we say of some excellent singer whose voice we have eulogized, "Hear and *see;*" or of a gem we have called very smooth, "Feel and *see.*" In a *new sense*, "It is *all in your eye.*"

Now all this use of terms arises from the fact that we *think by images, by something we can see* or *imagine that we see.* When a matter is clear to us, whether spoken or pictured, we cry,

OH, I SEE.

This characteristic of the mind makes "the likes" necessary in every kind of teaching. The unknown must be taught by likening it to something that is known; the unseen must be represented by the seen.

Eye-Teaching is also Scriptural.

Dr. Vincent, in the preface to his recent work on "The Church School," says: "The good philanthropists of the last century, in digging that they might build a human fabric, laid bare an ancient and divine foundation." These words, spoken of the modern Sunday School, are especially true of its eye-teaching.

It is not a "new idea," but an "ancient and divine foundation" laid bare for us to build upon to-day.

The Bible is full of object lessons taught by God Himself, by Christ, and by the inspired writers, with trees, stars, shields, girdles, fruits, birds, pictures, &c., as their texts and illustrations.

Eye-Teaching is adapted to the Times.

We need only refer to the increased amount of blackboard work in our day schools, to the large number of magazines and papers that have recently introduced illustrations in their hitherto unillustrated pages, to the inscriptions on boardings and fences, the great number of picture advertisements in our papers, and the increasing custom of our illustrating lectures, to remind our readers that one marked characteristic of this age is to put things into the mind by a quick concentration on the eye. We must "discern the signs of the times," and keep up with them. We must study times and men. The advertising pages, which are epitomized photographs of the day, and the "Bitters" on stones, "Pills" on trees, and "Magic Oil" on everything, notwithstanding their quackery, teach us that this age must be reached very much through the eye.

Divisions of the Whole Subject.

We make the divisions of the subject that follow, on the basis of their relative simplicity.

(I.) Vivid Description and Allegory.

A Bible scene is sometimes so vividly described, that it becomes eye-teaching, and stands before the scholar as a real picture.

(II.) Stories Vividly Told.

A story vividly narrated is a picture, and few scholars can carry ideas in any other way so well as in a mental picture.

(III.) Stories Represented.

Many stories may be made a little dramatic, or, at least, more vivid, by showing some prominent object mentioned in them, while the story is being told.

(IV.) Object Illustrations.*

The most perfect religious object lesson is like a mirror, the object itself but little noticed while it reflects some great truth.

---

* The following object illustrations were described by Mrs. W. F. Crafts:—
When teaching that the pillar of fire was light to the Israelites, but darkness to the Egyptians in crossing the Red Sea, show a piece of paper red on one side and black on the other. When this lesson was taught in my class, I provided each one of my assistants with such a piece of paper.

When telling about the rainbow as a sign of the covenant between God and man, have a prism to throw the colors on the wall, where they can remain while you talk about them. Get the children to move their hands in the shape of the rainbow.

In teaching about a walled city, Jericho, for instance, set up a toy village with a high row of blocks around it, and explain the similarities and contrast between the toy city and the walled city.

In teaching about the twelve stones which were set up in Gilgal as a monument of God's mercies to the Israelites, and applying the same thought to our remembrance of God's mercies to us, procure twelve marble chips. Write on them: Jesus Christ, The Comforter, The Bible, Heaven, Life, Prayer, Forgiveness, Home, Friends, Reason, Food, Clothing, and let them be set up as a monument before the class.

Illustrate the blessing of sight by showing an opera glass and telling what it enables us to do. Show how it must be regulated, then tell that each child has a more wonderful pair of glasses, with which he can see things both near and far, and which are self-regulating, self-cleansing, and beautiful in color. Tell the children that these "glasses" are their eyes.

The teacher should endeavor to give the Golden Text in some attractive form each week. For instance. "Who hath measured the waters in the hollow of his hand, and meted out heaven with a span," could be written on a hand cut out of paper, and given to each child. The Golden Text, "This beginning of miracles did Jesus in Cana of Galilee, and manifested forth his glory, and his disciples believed on him," could be written on a jar cut out of paper, and given to each child.

(V.) MAP TEACHING.

(VI.) PICTURE TEACHING.

(VII.) THE BLACKBOARD.

The blackboard excels the other forms of eye-teaching, in convenience, availability, and cheapness. Descriptions and stories require more time to introduce a thought into the mind than does the blackboard exercise. An object lesson, as a rule, can be used but once; the blackboard may be used again and again without sameness. A picture has but one surface, and that is soon familiar; the blackboard presents a new surface, a new picture, every time it is used. Maps are expensive, and many schools cannot afford but one; the blackboard may be made a series of maps, each of them new, with especial emphasis on the scene of the lesson.

THE ABUSES OF THE BLACKBOARD.

(1.) **Making an exhibition** of it rather than an illustration of truth by it.

(2.) **Incorrect Drawing.**

(3.) **Complicated Follies,** chiefly remarkable for ingenuity and emphasising unimportant syllables and letters.

USES OF THE BLACKBOARD.

(1.) **To collect attention.**
(2.) **To make announcements.**
(3.) **To aid the Memory.**
(4.) **To explain** truth.
(5.) **To condense thought.**
(6.) **To emphasize truth.**
(7.) **To review the lessons.**

The materials wanted are a blackboard or a strip of blackboard cloth,* a box of crayons, and a good eraser.

The teacher's slate, which may be used in each class as effectively and variously as the blackboard in the general school.

Thus we have spoken of the seven departments of eye-teaching.

They should ever be as the seven golden candlesticks of Revelation, not attracting the eyes of men to themselves, but only revealing the glory of Him who cried from their midst,

"I AM ALPHA AND OMEGA,

THE BEGINNING AND THE ENDING,

THE FIRST AND THE LAST."

---

12. IMPORTANCE AND METHOD OF PUBLIC REVIEWS.

BY REV. J. L. HURLBUT.

(1.) A public review **brings the mind anew in contact with Divine Truth.**

(2.) Imparts a **clearer understanding of the lesson**.

(3.) **Deepens the impression** on the heart.

(4.) Presents **new aspects of the truth**.

(5.) **Aids the memory** in retaining the lesson.

(6.) **Illustrates methods** of teaching.

(7.) **Reproves the inefficient teachers**.

(8.) **Supplements the deficiencies** of class-teaching.

(9.) **Gives both variety and unity** to the exercises.

---

* A former obstacle to the general use of the blackboard was its expensiveness. This exists no longer, as a strip of *blackboard cloth* can be purchased for about a dollar, large enough for a good blackboard, and either hung up as a map, or nailed to an easel. This blackboard cloth is sent by mail by the manufacturers, "The Silicate Slate Co.," corner of Church and Fulton Sts., New York. Send for circulars. For sale also by Adam Miller & Co., Toronto.

Third Quarter, 1876.

Among other pleasant devices for a review is the above blackboard picture of a shelf of twelve books,* to be drawn on a blackboard at the beginning of the Quarter with blank backs. In the closing review let the initials of the lesson subject ("David's charge to Solomon" in this case) be printed after it has been given by the school; also in the same way the initials of the topic (in this case, in Berean Series, "Ministry to God divinely appointed"); also the outline (Ministry to God appointed—Why—How—"); also the first word of the Golden Text ("Know thou the God of thy father, &c.,"); also the "Doctrine" (God a Sovereign). Each Sunday's review fills up an additional book, and **the previous ones should be reviewed each time**, so that, at the end of the Quarter, with the help of these initials and these weekly reviews, the subjects, topics, outlines, golden texts and the doctrines of the twelve lessons can be given by the school. One blackboard, or at least one side of a blackboard must be set aside for this one purpose in this plan. For variety these initials can sometimes be put in twelve picture frames, or twelve scrolls, drawn upon the blackboard in a similar way.

---

13. What the Sunday School can Learn from the Public School.

BY JAMES HUGHES.†

One is almost led to believe sometimes, that Sunday School

---

* Original with Mrs. S. W. Clark, of Newark.
† Inspector of Public Schools, Toronto.

teachers *can* learn very little. Like the good old Scotch lady, who, when tea was first introduced poured out the *broth*, as she called it, and ate the cold tea leaves, they often use the various aids provided for them in a manner totally different from that which was intended by those who designed them. Take for instance the lesson papers. Did those who designed them expect, that in hundreds of Sunday Schools they would almost completely drive the Bible out of doors?

Did they imagine, that thousands of teachers would sit down before their classes every Sunday with these papers in their hands, and ask the questions literally as they appear in print?

Did they think, when they stated or referred to from forty to fifty facts on a lesson paper, that thousands of teachers would try every Sunday to force all these facts into the minds of their scholars in about thirty minutes, when it is well known that no teacher should or could teach more than eight or ten facts or thoughts in that time?

Nor do they err because they have not been taught better. I shall not, however, deal with the capacity of the learners, but merely with the lessons to be learned.

The first thing attended to in a well regulated Public School is Order. It is said that "Order is Heaven's first law. The teacher and heaven should be on a par in this respect. No teacher of good standing would think of *teaching* at all until he had established between himself and his class a perfect understanding regarding this matter; until he had clearly shown his pupils that it was necessary that one person should be absolutely master, and that he was the person entitled to that position by virtue of his office, his superior intelligence, experience, and force of character. Without order in his business and among his employees, no business man can hope to be successful. Without the perfect order which we call discipline in an army it is a disorganized mob, incapable, unmanageable, at the mercy of its foes. Without order in a school, at least one-half of a teacher's power is wasted, partly through the inattention of the scholars, and partly in reducing the disorder to what some teachers regard as endurable limits. Experience has proved this, and therefore every good teacher insists on having good order before attempting to teach.

Now if order is important in a Public School, how much more essential is it in a Sunday School, where the disorder of one class usually interferes so materially with the attention and progress of all the others. Yet it is astonishing how general the idea is that it is quite orthodox for Sunday School scholars to discuss all the events of the past week, and the probabilities for the week to come, while their teachers are talking to them about God's Word. It is astonishing, too, to see scholars, who sit during five days in the week in the Public School without uttering one whispered word to their seatmates, or even thinking of such an outrage, conversing as freely with their companions in Sunday School as if they were receiving visits at their own homes. But the most astonishing thing of all is that, among the thousands of Sunday School teachers, there are so few who either deem order to be indispensable, or have the force of character to insist on having it; and so many who are willing to sit listlessly before a class and talk on mechanically, knowing, as they must, that perhaps not a single individual is listening to what they say. When such is the case I do not wonder that the scholars amuse themselves. On the teachers I lay all the blame. The scholars accept matters as they find them. Teachers must be weak indeed if the scholars form public opinion in a school, and establish its character. Some teachers try to excuse themselves by saying that if they insist on having precise order, their scholars will leave them. No greater mistake could be made. Children like order better than disorder. So would all grown people if they had been properly trained at school. Children are most joyous and happy, and, of course, most thoroughly educated in those Public Schools where the discipline is strict without being severe. There is no quicker way for a teacher to lose the respect of his pupils than by overindulging them. I can sympathize, however, with a rational teacher who has a class in an ordinary Sunday School. It is a difficult matter for one person to stem the torrent under such circumstances. One of my Public School teachers while endeavoring to secure attention in her Sunday School class was met with the remark, from a young lady of fifteen; "You need not think that you are going to get us to behave in Sunday School as your scholars do in the Public School. Miss

—— (another teacher in the same Sunday School) says you are altogether too particular."

When I use the word "order" I do not wish to be understood to mean perfect quiet or stillness, I mean **the order of life, not the order of death,** I mean by *order* having every child and teacher and officer in a school attending to his own duty, and to that alone, and attending to it, of course, in the quietest possible manner. But so long as no individual in a school is attending to another's business, or doing anything simply to attract the attention of any person else, I would not sacrifice efficiency for the sake of silence, I would much prefer a good stiff breeze to a dead calm. The breeze is all right unless it comes in squalls. Perfect order may be quite in harmony with great noise. In a factory, for instance, although the noise of machinery may be deafening, and the bustle of the workmen quite confusing to an outsider, everything is usually in the most perfect order. The very fundamental principle of the Kintergarten schools may be said to be the use of the tendencies and actions of childhood in an orderly manner. In Sunday Schools as at present arranged it is impossible to have teaching going on without some noise, but this does not necessarily mean disorder. If one or two classes are taking the lead in making a noise, then there is disorder. If two or three scholars in a class are talking to themselves, or pushing, or throwing paper balls, lozenges, &c., or cutting the buttons off their teacher's coat, or sticking pins into the pupils in the next class, or pulling their hair, or reading song books during school hours, or doing anything calculated to distract the attention of others from their proper work, then there is disorder that should be checked immediately, checked before any more teaching should be attempted. When some of these practices are allowed in nearly every Sunday School; when it is deemed perfectly natural for scholars to engage in chit chat while God's Holy Word is being read, and even, while God is being addressed in prayer, I do not wonder that our children grow up with such an alarming lack of reverence for God's House, and God's Word. No wonder that in most churches flippant conversation is indulged in, and in some *advanced* places secular newspapers are read while waiting for the commencement of church services.

It is not within the scope of my subject to tell how order can most easily and most permanently be secured. I shall, however, mention several of the erroneous attempts made to obtain it in the Sunday School, and the remedies as practised in the Public School.

Perhaps no other aid is so frequently invoked, or so much relied on to maintain order in Sunday Schools as **the Superintendent's bell**. This was introduced from the Public School, but it is used in a manner that would not be sanctioned in any good Public School. The bell is a valuable aid to discipline. It may be used with great profit instead of the teacher's voice, as a signal for commencing, changing, or closing exercises, for standing up, sitting down, assembling, dismissing, &c., but it never should be used to give a command for order. I would regard any Public School Teacher as badly trained, if he rang his bell for any other purpose than as a time signal, or for the performance of mechanical movements. Of course the opening bell in a Sunday School may be regarded as an indirect signal for order, because it should be an understood fact that the school exercises would not commence until perfect quiet was secured. The idea of ringing a bell several times, and excitedly accompanying the action with cries of "order," "order," is too ridiculous for any trained or thoughtful man to think of for an instant. I would as soon expect to put out a fire with coal oil, or calm a nervous child by firing cannons near it, as to obtain order in that way. Even the occasional ringing of the bell for order is an error. It disturbs every class in the room, while perhaps only one or two are offending, and after a time loses its effect, because it speaks directly to no one, and gives in general terms, and to a whole class, instructions that ought to be given particularly to certain individuals. In general terms the following rule may be followed with reference to the bell :—It should never convey a command that does not apply with equal force to each member of the school.

Sunday Schools may learn a lesson from the Public Schools in regard to the number of pupils to place in charge of one teacher. A Sunday School of three hundred scholars has, as a rule, about thirty-five teachers, while a Public School with the same number would have six or seven teachers. I have no hesitation in saying that I firmly believe the teaching power of the Sunday School would be greatly increased by a reduction in the number of teachers in it to something near the Public School standard. It is at present, and will long continue to be, an impossibility to find thirty-five first class teachers in a congregation representing three hundred Sunday School children. But every congregation ought to be able to turn out from six to ten persons who *can teach ;* teach in the true sense of the term, not merely take charge of classes. Of course with this number of teachers I would have **each class in a separate room**, so that there would be much less to attract the attention of the pupils, and consequently the order would be much more easily maintained. There is no doubt that the very fact of being in a room somewhat similar in style to their ordinary schoolrooms, would dispose the scholars to be more orderly, and induce a frame of mind favorable to the reception of knowledge. Each teacher too would have perfect freedom of voice, action, and manner, and would be at liberty to use, without annoying others, blackboard, maps, illustrations, diagrams, specimens, &c. He could be a real, live, standing, walking, talking, energetic, magnetic teacher, freed from all the cramps and restraints of a room in which there are several teachers. **Give one of the best eight Teachers in a Sunday School of three hundred pupils, forty of them in a room of their own**, and if they are of about the same state of advancement, he must be a good deal of what we call a "stick" if he cannot instruct each of them thoroughly, and keep them interested with less strain on himself, and more success, than he would have in teaching eight in a large room when surrounded by other classes, who were continually annoying him, and whom he was continually afraid of annoying. Of course, he would have to vary his mode of proceeding in such circumstances. He could **not do so much individual teaching** with forty as with eight. It would not be necessary to do so much under such circumstances. I knew a good old gentleman, who was placed in charge of about forty boys, and in a short time he came to me complaining that by the time he called the roll and heard each boy recite his verses, the time had arrived for closing. I was not surprised at that; neither was I surprised to find, that the last twenty-five boys having heard the verses repeated and re-repeated so often, were able to answer very correctly, when their turn came, without having previously studied the lesson at all; nor was I surprised to find, that there was a great deal of disorder amongst those who had to recite first and then amuse themselves while the others were doing their part. No trained teacher would make such a mistake as that. They could each be tested as to their knowledge of the verses to be recited, and their recitation or failures marked, in less than ten minutes, by any teacher of ordinary ability.

"But," some will say, "we have not got accommodation for such an arrangement of classes." If not, you can have. If you can seat three hundred scholars in a room where they are subdivided into thirty or forty classes, I can seat four hundred comfortably in the same room **partitioned into eight class-rooms.** There is really a large amount of seating space lost, usually by the small class method. "Our Sunday School," you say, "is not arranged with that end in view." Alter it by **sliding or folding partitions, or even curtains.** "We are in the basement and could not get light for the central rooms," others say. Get out of the basement. The sooner the better. If you cannot do so, make the upper half of your partitions of glass. But it is worth while to try very hard to get out of the basement ?

But the Sunday School should learn to decrease the number in a class as well as increase. Many infant classes are mere masses of panting little darlings, who are compelled to fight for breathing space and elbow room, while their unfortunate teachers are vainly endeavoring to explain to them the love of Jesus. I have frequently seen from one hundred to two hundred children in one infant class under one teacher. This is a more monstrous error than the one already discussed. Such a class should be divided into at least three or four parts, or use Mrs. Craft's plan of assistant teachers. "Oh, but," some Superintendents say, "we have difficulty in obtaining *one* successful infant class teacher." No wonder. Put four hundred in a class, and your difficulty will be vastly increased. I would expect to have difficulty in obtaining a person, who could manage and teach two hundred little folks even in a suitable room, but I would readily undertake to find four persons in a large congregation, who could each do justice to fifty of them. In the Kintergarten Schools, taught by ladies of vast training and experience, the usual number in charge of a teacher is twenty, and the utmost limit twenty-five. The legal number for each teacher in Ontario Public Schools is fifty. In most cities of the United States it is less than fifty. Whatever may be the size of the class in charge of a teacher, there is another important lesson for Sunday Schools to learn from Secular Schools. **A teacher should always see all of his scholars.** In Public Schools care is taken to have a platform for the teacher, so that he may be able from his elevated position to see the whole school. He is even instructed while attending his Normal School to acquire his profession, to stand with his right side to the black-board, when writing on it, so that he may the more readily sweep his eye over his class. How vastly different is the practice of hundreds of Sunday School teachers! How calmly they seat themselves, Sunday after Sunday, as close as possible to the central pupils in their classes, quite oblivious to the fact, that they have scholars behind them on each side, who are left to amuse themselves by such plans as their ingenuity may devise. A teacher in such a position always suggests to me the idea of a man attempting to fill some pails with water by placing the pails behind the pump instead of under the spout. The pails would get as much good as the pupils, and do far less mischief.

Sunday School Teachers should learn not to ask questions to their pupils in rotation. Many commence at the head of the class facing the pupil there, and after putting him through, as though he were the only pupil in the class, they shift their chairs and get over number two in a similar manner, and so on to the end of the class, if happily that part be reached before closing time. They can teach but one at a time. If the lessons of the Bible were arranged to correspond with the order of the pupils in the class, so that each one might get the lesson he specially needed, this might not be so completely ridiculous a method. But Tom may receive Harry's lesson, Harry, Fred's, and so on. **No pupil should ever know who is likely to receive a question until it**

has been given. No name should be mentioned, no motion made, or look given to indicate who is to answer, until the question has been asked. Each pupil should know that he may be asked every question. Every one will thus be compelled to attend all the time, while if questions are asked in rotation, a pupil, after answering his question, may discuss the circus, or the last lacrosse match, or the next base ball match, or any other *appropriate* Sunday School topic, that may chance to come into his mind, until his turn is coming again. If I had a teacher who insisted on sitting squarely in front of each pupil in turn, I would accommodate his class to his capacity, by giving him *one small scholar,* so that he might see the whole of his class at once.

Sunday School Teachers should learn not to repeat their questions for the sake of those who do not hear them the first time. It is simply an extra inducement to the scholars to be inattentive to do so. If a pupil knows that your question is only to be asked once, he will listen to it the first time. If he knows that, when you wish him to answer, you will shake him to get his attention, and then repeat your question, he will wait for his shaking.

Sunday School Teachers should learn not to stare fixedly at the pupil who is reading or answering. If there is one pupil who does not need watching, he is that one. He is certain to be attending to his work. We should attend to him with the ear, to all others with the eye.

Public School experience has demonstrated clearly that, **telling is not teaching.** Lecturing or sermonizing is not teaching. The teacher should lead or guide his pupils through the garden of knowledge, and show them which kinds of fruit are beneficial, and which injurious; he should also show them the best means for obtaining the fruit, but he should not pluck it for them, and eat it for them, and digest it for them. The teacher should **teach his scholars how to think**; he should not do the thinking for them.

Sunday School teachers should learn to give an introduction to, or explanation of, the lesson for next Sunday. We have been learning during the past few years, that one of our most important duties as Public School teachers is to **teach children how to study,** and what to study most carefully in connection with each lesson. It is a very important point. To assign a lesson to a child without giving him some idea of what are its leading features ; what you will expect him to know, or explain, or prove next Sunday ; and how and where he can obtain most light on difficult parts, seems to me to be a good deal **like sending him into a ten acre swamp to fetch something he has never seen, and which you have not even described to him.** Lesson papers, when properly used, do a good deal towards the accomplishment of this object, but they require explanation and weeding out, as they frequently contain matter that most teachers will not need to use. I would make the lesson paper the basis of my outline or framework of next Sunday's lesson, but I would eliminate from and add to it in order to adapt to the special requirements or advancement of my class. I would allow my scholars to take out their lesson papers and lead pencils at the close of the lesson of the day, to mark them according to my directions. With a lesson thus definitely set before them, scholars will be much more interested, than when they are told simply the portion of Scripture which is to constitute the lesson, or else "to get what is on the lesson paper." It is the great duty of the teacher to make the text book or lesson paper, or whatever he places in the hands of his scholars comprehensible to them, and all recognised authorities agree, that this should be done before the lesson is studied, so far as mapping out the work to be done is concerned.

Most Sunday School teachers need to learn, that **children under fourteen years of age require a great deal of explanation,** far more than at first sight seems reasonable. Adults who are not in the habit of associating with children every day, are liable to shoot over their heads altogether, when they come to teach them. Even Public School teachers usually take a long time to learn to be simple enough in their language and illustrations, and clear and definite enough in their explanations. It is so difficult for us to remember or comprehend the change that has taken place in our mental power since we were children. He is certain to be the best teacher, who has the most vivid recollections of his own childhood. Of course the amount of explanation necessary will depend to a certain extent upon the social condition of the children, and the character of the Public Schools which they attend; but every man will make a better teacher if he will repeat to himself every day before commencing his duties; "*I must remember that, as an adult I am disposed to pass over as simple much that my scholars do not understand, and to make use of reasonings and language above their comprehension.*" Another lesson of a kindred character that may be learned from the experience of Public School teachers is, **not to expect your pupils to progress too rapidly,** or to remember too long what they have been taught, and not to be discouraged, if they do not seem to remember anything at all. It is the hardest and most humiliating of all the lessons a teacher has to learn that, a month after he has patiently and clearly explained some difficult matter to his class, they have almost, if not altogether, forgotten it. Such, however, is the fact of the matter, but instead of being discouraged, a teacher should let this lesson teach him two others; 1st, **not to attempt to teach too much**, and 2nd, **to repeat and review more persistently**. These are two of the most important things for a Public School teacher to attend to, and they are neglected in Sunday Schools more uniformly than any that I have mentioned. A child might nearly as well undertake to swallow the mighty St. Lawrence, as it rolls so majestically on, as try to take in the torrents of dates, historical facts, geographical facts, illustrations, explanations, reasonings, conclusions, &c., &c., that are poured out to them promiscuously by many teachers. I am well aware that the cry used to be from many teachers, "We cannot get enough to keep our classes occupied." This will always be the experience of those individuals who do not prepare their lessons, but I do not regard them as teachers. Their millenium passed away with the introduction of the uniform lessons, and their shortening to a few verses, instead of a few chapters. My first Sunday School teacher, in the palmy days, when each teacher selected his own portion of Scripture, always avoided becoming exhausted, by commencing so far from the end of the Bible, that we could not possibly finish it before the close of school. My experience with Sunday School teachers leads me to believe that, when their lessons contain a reasonable number of points it is the result of necessity rather than choice. The evil that I speak of has been necessarily increased by the publication of such a number of lesson notes and papers. Many teachers in their use of these remind me of the old New Englander who was always complaining that his sons were idle and slow in doing their work, and urging them to greater exertions by telling them how "the young men used to work when he was young." One day when his sons were drawing in hay, the old gentleman came out to see how they were getting along, and as usual commenced to declaim about the contrast between *his* sons, and those of his father. "Why," said he, "when I was young I could build a load of hay as fast as three men could pitch it." Tired out with his continual prating, his sons informed him, that they believed two of them could pitch hay faster than he could build it, and the old gentleman could not do otherwise than except their challenge or else "forever hold his peace." He chose the former alternative, mounted the wagon, and shouted "Hay!" His sons responded with a will. Straining muscles and forkhandles, they threw up the hay so rapidly, that he could barely climb over it and trample it down. Yet he continued valiantly to call out, "More hay! More hay!" And they gave him more. Quicker and larger came the bundles, so quickly, and so large, that he was sometimes more than half buried. Still he continued bravely. Panting with his exertions, he would climb, and tramp, and shout, "More hay! More hay! Don't go asleep, boys! More hay, I tell you!" But his load looked like a pile of hay blown together by a whirlwind. It had no proper foundation or any regular shape, and at length it and the old gentleman rolled over, and came tumbling to the ground. Now was the complete triumph of his sons. They ran around just in time to find him crawling out from under the pile of hay; and with mock gravity enquired: "What did you come down for father?" "What did I come down for," he thundered, "Why I came down for MORE HAY!" There are a great many Sunday School teachers who prepare their lessons as the old grumbler built his load of hay. They pitchfork into their note books all the ideas they can find in the Presbyterian Journals, the Methodist Journals, the Baptist Journals, the Congregational Journals, the Non-Denominational Journals, the Commentaries, the Histories, the Geographies, &c., and then they look for more. Yes, and when Sunday comes they sit down before their classes, open their bag of miscellaneous extracts, and proceed to hand them out as they come without arrangement or connection. They rake together the thoughts of several men, and attempt to give the whole mass as a lesson. The result is, the memories of the children are overwhelmed, and their minds confused. Why, not one of the gentlemen who prepare these lesson notes, would attempt to teach all that he himself publishes in his notes. These notes are not given as lessons, but as material from which to form lessons. I am very far from finding fault with any teacher for getting all the information possible in relation to the lesson. It is highly commendable, and to maintain your proper standing with thoughtful and intelligent pupils, it is absolutely necessary to do so. But for every hour devoted to the accumulation of matter for the lesson, two should be given to the arrangement of **the method of teaching it**. Any one can get a mass of facts and thoughts on the lesson, but very few comparatively can reject what is unnecessary, and wisely select and arrange that which they require for their particular classes.

However, if every teacher taught *well* and gave his scholars a reasonable amount in each lesson, they would not remember what they were taught, without **constant repetition and reviewing**. There is no word in the teacher's guide-book so important as the word REPEAT. How often did you repeat your multiplication table before you learned it? You repeated it until it became a part of your very nature. There is not much learned so thoroughly as that in the Sunday School. This is, in my opinion, the weakest point in connection with Sunday-school teaching. It is the opening in the wall through which oceans of earnest effort flow without effect. To teach without reviewing is to scatter seed without harrowing it into the ground, so that it does not germinate, but is eaten by the birds. "Well," some one says, "we do have reviews in our Sunday Shool. The Superintendent reviews the lesson after it is taught every Sunday." No doubt; that is one of the fundamental principles in nearly every Sunday School. The idea was obtained from the Public Schools; but it is another instance of pouring out the "broth" and eating the cold tea leaves. I never could understand how this custom could have become so universal, or why, if indulged in at all, the Superintendent's "few remarks" should be called a review. That a review is attempted, however, shows that the necessity for it is acknowledged by all. The questions that need to be settled there are, "What is the best time for reviewing?" and "Who should be the reviewer?" Experience in the Public Schools answers these questions most unmistakably, and without any hesitation or reservation. The proper time to review the lesson of to-day is immediately before teaching the lesson of to-morrow on the same subject. The proper person to do the reviewing is the one who taught the lesson to be reviewed and is going to teach the next. Re-teaching the lesson, as done in Sunday Schools generally at the close of the teacher's work, does no harm, if the Superintendent is not too prosy; but it does not do enough good. It is just when a lesson is slipping out of the memory that it should be reviewed. If Public School teachers find it necessary to review the lesson of one day before continuing the same subject on the next, how much more will it be necessary for the Sunday School teacher to do so after a week has passed? The reviewing then, done in a very few minutes, brings all the essential points of the last lesson before the minds of the scholars, and thus forms a proper basis for the lesson of the day. That the proper reviewer is the teacher is evident, when we reflect that no other person can know so well how much his class should answer, or what he is going to teach. On these two things should depend the nature and extent of the review. I would not recommend a teacher as the examiner of his own class; but an examination and a review are entirely different things. It is not enough, however, for a teacher to review the lesson once as already suggested; he should **review regularly while teaching**. A good Public School teacher will not give more than about three facts to a class without questioning his class to see that they are remembered. He will then discuss a couple more, and drill over the whole five given; then teach a couple more and examine on the seven, and so on to the end. "Oh, I would never get over my lesson in that way" will, no doubt, be said. Very well; your object should not be to "get over the lesson," but to teach it." Your teaching cannot be measured by the amount you "get over," but by the amount which your pupils remember and apply. In Sunday Schools, as at present constituted, it may be advisable to have the reviewing done by the Superintendent or Pastor, but they should review last Sunday's lesson before the commencement of the lesson for the day.

I have referred incidentally to the indolent class of persons whose consciences allow them to sit down before their classes on Sunday without preparing their lessons, or perhaps even knowing where the lesson is. A Public School teacher who would act in such a manner would have a lively time. If he were married his furniture would not last long. He would belong to the migratory species. **A live Public School teacher would not think of using a Text-Book while teaching** history, grammar, geography, or geometry, or in explaining the rules of arithmetic or algebra. Even in teaching a reading lesson, I would expect him to be able to give most of his attention to the class, and yet correct all the errors made, in pronunciation, punctuation, emphasis, &c. It would be a great thing if Sunday School teachers would all imitate such an example. I do not mean to say that I would like to see the Bible, the Sunday School Text-Book, banished from the class, or disused either by teacher or scholars. It should be there for reference use; it should be there in order to teach the scholars how to use it properly, to give them a due reverence for it, and to keep the idea prominently before them, that the Sunday School is a Bible School. It would be a great change for the better, however, if every Sunday School teacher would go to his or her class prepared to close the Bible so far as the lesson itself is concerned. If teachers knew their lessons, they would not need so constantly and so unsuccessfully to urge their scholars to learn them.

Sunday Schools should learn and are learning to have trained teachers. Whatever may be the natural gifts a man or woman may have for any position, he or she will be infinitely better fitted to perform its duties after a systematic training for it. A man may have a natural taste and aptness for the practice of medicine, but not many of us would trust our lives in his hands to be experimented upon, unless he had taken his degree.

Similar remarks may be made with equal force in relation to a lawyer in connection with business transactions, or difficulties. Why, it requires a training even to fit a young lady to keep house properly. I read of a young wife recently, who had been educated at a fashionable boarding school, whose husband requested her one morning to order their dinner, as he was too busy to do so as usual. Her order to the butcher was, " A leg of tongue, 17lbs. steak, and two Halibut." The most enlightened countries of the world, Prussia, Switzerland, the British Isles, the United States and Canada, have the best facilities for turning out a constant supply of well-trained teachers. Taking the United States individually, it will be found that the people are the most intelligent in those States where the institutions for **teacher training** are most numerous and most complete. If the Sunday School is to keep pace with the progress of the age; if it is going to exercise its due influence in moulding the characters of the men and women of the future; if it is going to be the power for good, which it should be, its teachers must not only be thoroughly taught in Bible truths, and those which relate to them, but trained in the correct principles of teaching.

I believe that the time will soon arrive when the Sunday School will imitate the Public School by having **written examinations**. No examination, written or oral, can thoroughly test the amount of work done by a good teacher; he is but a half-hearted teacher whose chief aim in teaching is to make his pupils pass a good examination; but written examinations have been found very beneficial in connection with Public Schools, and I am convinced they would be equally valuable in Sunday Schools. They materially induce teachers and scholars to greater effort; they make the teaching more pointed and less diffuse, and they lead to more systematic and thorough reviewing. A written examination of their pupils on the work of the past six months would teach most teachers a serious lesson. These examinations should be held twice a year. The examination papers might be prepared by the Committee of the local Sunday School Associations in cities and towns, or by the Provincial or State Association, or by committees appointed by denominational publishing houses. In the latter cases it would be necessary to have the examinations in all parts on the same day. In either case the cost would be trifling. I have not time to discuss the method of conducting them, but merely throw out these suggestions as seed thoughts, regarding a subject which must soon engross the attention of Sunday School workers.

Lastly, I would like to see **Sunday Schools placed on the same footing financially with relation to the Church that Public Schools hold towards the municipalities**, and the State. On the plea that the education given by the Public Schools is for the benefit of the State, the State provides the Public School authorities with the funds necessary for carrying on their work. Does not the Sunday School bear even a closer relation to the Church than the Public School does to the State? Is it not literally a department, aye, and an important department, of the Church? Why then should it not have its place in the Church estimates? Why should the teachers and officers who give their time to teach the children of the Church be compelled to beg for the money to provide their school requisites?

In discussing my subject I have not touched upon the great fundamental principles of teaching, which the most advanced Public School teachers endeavour to practise. Every Sunday School teacher, who desires to commence the real study of the science of childhood should read the works of Pestalozzi and Froebel, those patient, loving, pioneers, who were the first men, since Christ, who penetrated very far into the realms of childhood.

14. A STUDY OF CHRIST AS THE MODEL TEACHER.

BY REV. F. H. MARLING.

It is important to success in any enterprise that we should have the most perfect example in every particular as our model.

In the Bible we have a perfect model of a teacher placed before us. We direct your attention—

First, to the fact, **Jesus did teach** ! He gave an example. See John xiii. 13, 15. He is called " the Word," John i. 1, &c. ; and a word is a channel of communication of thought from one mind to another. John i. 18 ; "declared" the Father, Gen. xlix. 10; Deut. xviii. 15, 19 ; Psalm xl. 6, 10 ; Isa. lxi. 1, 3. Applied by Jesus himself, Luke iv. 16, 24.

Succession and contrast. Heb. i, 1, 2 ; Repeatedly spoke of his mission thus, John xviii. 37 ; Luke iv. 42, 43.

Why did Jesus teach ? 1. Work given him of God. Matt. xvii. 5 ; John v. 30 ; John vii. 16, 18 ; John viii. 2, 6.

2. Because he loved it for the truth's sake and souls. Psalm x. 4-8 ; John iv. 31, 34 ; Mark vi. 34 ; Mark x. 21 ; Matt. xxiii. 37.

Whom did he teach? Generally his own people. Matt. xv. 24, 25, 28 ; Matt. x. 5, 6 ; Matt. viii. 10, 13.

All whom he could reach. Matt. iv. 12, 23, 24, 25 ; Matt xi. 1 ; Mark i. 33.

Where did he teach? In the synagogue, sea-side, &c. John iii. 17 ; John iv. 6, 19 ; Luke x. 38, 42 ; Luke xxiv. 13, 15.

Where greatest need—most teachable spirit. Matt. ix. 13 ; John xvi. 12.

Even his enemies. John ix. 39, 41.

What did he teach ? Moral and scriptural truths of the Old Testament. Matt. xv. 2, 6 ; Matt. iv. 4, 7, 10 ; Matt. xii. 3, 5 ; Matt. xxii. 29, 32 ; Luke x. 25, 28 ; Matt. xxvi. 53, 56 ; Luke xxiv. 25, 27, 44, 48 ; Matt. xv., xxiii.

Taught of Himself. Matt. x. 27, 30 ; John iii. 14, 16 ; John v. 17, 29 ; John vi. 26, 40 ; John x. 1, 18 ; John xi. 25, 27 ; John xiv. 15, 16.

How ? 1. *After ample previous preparation ?* Luke ii. 40, 52. Lived and practised the truth thirty years. Luke iii. 23.

2. Out of a large human experience.—Heb. iv. 14, 16 ; Heb. ii. 17, 18 ; Heb. v. 1, 2 ; Heb. x. 7, 9.

3. *Fulness of Spirit.* Isa. xli. 1, 3 ; Isa. xi. 1, 5 ; Luke i. 35. Luke iii. 21, 22 ; Luke iv. 1, 2, 14 ; John iii. 34 ; 1 Cor. ii. 4. 16.

4. *Weight and certainty.* Matt. v. 22, 28, 32, 34, 39 ; Matt. vii. 28, 29 ; John iii. 11, 13 ; John ix. 4, 5 ; 1 Cor. xiv. 37.

5. *With all his might?* John ix. 45 ; John xi. 8, 9 ; Matt. xiv. 13, 25.

6. *With loving kindness.* Isa. xl. 11 ; Psalm lxxii. 12, 14 ; Luke iv. 22 ; Mark x. 15, 16 ; Matt. xviii. 10, 14 ; Luke vii. 35, 60 ; John xi. 33, 36.

7. *Fearless and faithful.* Matt. xi. 20 ; Matt. xxiii. 13 ; Matt. xv. 7, 14.

8. *It was steeped in prayer.* Luke iv. 21, 22 ; Luke vi. 12, 13 ; Matt. xiv. 22, 23 ; Luke ix. 28 ; John xi. 41, 43 ; Luke xxii. 31, 32 ; Heb. v. 7, 8 ; John xvii. 12 ; John ix. 11, 17.

9. *Plain and simple.* Matt. xi. 26 ; Mark xii. 27 ; John vii. 14, 15 ; John iii. 12 ; John xvi. 12, 13 ; Matt. xvi. 6, 12.

10. *Abounded with illustration.* Matt. vi. 1, 4 ; Matt. v. 15 ; Matt. xvi. 18 ; Matt, xxvi. 30 ; Matt. vii, 24, 27 ; Matt. xiii. 1, 8.

11. *Object lesson.* Little child in midst of disciples. "Penny." "Seest thou this woman."

12. *Employed questions.* Addressed reason. Luke ii. 46, 49 ; Luke vi. 8, 9 ; Luke x. 25, 37 ; Matt. xxii. 15, 52.

13. *Much repetition.* Isa. xxviii. 9, 13 ; Matt. xiii. 51, 52 ; Matt. vi. 2, 15, 16 ; Matt. vii. 7 ; Mark ix. 43, 48.

14. *Very flexible and various.* John iv. ; Matt. xxii.

15. *The word was accompanied with works of grace.* Matt. iv. 23, 24 ; Matt. xi. 1, 6 ; Mark vi. 54, 56 ; Mark iii. 7, 10.

16. What followed his teaching ?

   1. *Popular attention and interest.* Matt. vii. 28, 29 ; Matt. xxi. 7, 11 ; Mark vi. 2 ; Mark xi. 18 ; Luke iv. 32 ; Luke xix. 47, 48 ; John vii. 11, 13, 45, 49.

   2. *Many souls won.* John iv. 1 ; John i. 40, 41, 43, 49 ; John x. 25, 27 ; John xii. 10, 11 ; Matt. xvi. 13, 17.

3. *Many hardened*—Some "went back." Luke ii. 34, 35; Luke iv. 28, 29; Mark ii. 5, 6, John v. 16, 18; Luke vii. 11.

4. *Noble band of helpers was raised up.* Matt. x. 1; Luke vi. 12, 17; Luke x. 1, 2; Luke ix. 49, 50; Acts iv. 27, 33; Acts i. 4, 8.

5. *Teaching with power.* John xii. 23, 24; John iv. 10, 13, 14; John vii. 37, 39; John vi. 47, 51.

---

15. SPIRITUAL WORK IN THE SUNDAY SCHOOL.

BY REV. B. P. RAYMOND.

The most important agent in the spiritual work of the Sunday School is the Holy Spirit. As teachers it becomes us to know well *His mission* and *His methods*.

I. **His Mission**:

(*a*) To **convict** of sin. See John xvi. 8.

(*b*) To **beget the soul anew** in Christ Jesus. See John iii. 5.

II. **His Method**:

(*a*) Is that of **a person**. Read the fourteenth chapter of John, and mark the fact that the Spirit is ever a "He," not an "It;" a "Who," not a "What"—a person and not a thing.

(*b*) Is that of **a Divine person**. See Acts v. 3, 4.

(*c*) The Divine works through **the media of truth**. 1. Of **truths of nature**.—See Rom. i. 20. 2. But especially of **truths of Revelation**.—See John xvii. 17. 3. And more especially still through the most potent truth on earth, viz., **the consecrated heart**. See 1 Cor. vi. 19.

16. Sunday School Teachers' Decalogue.

By Rev. E. O. Haven, D.D., LLD.

1. Pray for inspiration, wisdom and patience.
    2 Timothy ii. 24; James i. 5.
2. Have faith in your convictions.
    Mark xi. 22; John xiv. 1; Hebrews xi. 32, 33.
3. Respect your pupils.
    Luke xi. 11; Matthew x. 29, 31.
4. Understand your own purpose.
    Proverbs xvii. 24; Luke vi. 39.
5. Obtain the attention and affection of your pupils.
    Matthew vii. 6, 9, 10; 1 Thessalonians ii. 7, 8.
6. Express thought precisely; illustrate freely.
    1 Corinthians xiv. 19; Matthew xiii. 34.
7. Teach arrangement and classification.
    2 Tim. ii. 15; Eccles. iii. 1 and 11.
8. Christ's test; fruit.
    Matthew vii. 16–20.
9. Review frequently.
    Isaiah xxv iii. 10.
10. Expect great results.
    Ecclesiastes xi. 1; Matthew xiii. 8.

"Thou, therefore, which teachest another, teachest thou not thyself?"

---

17. Five Elements of Success in Teaching.

By Rev. Richard Newton, D.D.

1. A real, heartfelt, glowing love for children.
2. A habit of forming a clear and distinct idea of the subject.
3. A simple, natural and well-defined plan.
4. Simplicity of language and directness of illustration.
5. Earnest piety.

18. FOR PREACHERS AND TEACHERS.

☞ TO BE COPIED AND HUNG ON YOUR DESK.

PREPARATION.

PROVING.
PAINTING.
PERSUADING.

"I am resolved to spare no pains, nor toil, nor time in *careful preparation*, in making my descriptions *graphic*, my *statements lucid*, my *appeals pathetic*, in filling my discourse in fact with what would both *strike and stick*."
—*Guthrie.*

"He should not merely prepare his sermon; he should also prepare himself."
—*Dr. Parker.*

UTTERANCE.

Manner is to
Matter, as powder to ball.

"CULTIVATE THE PAUSE, SIR."

"When you read the Sacred Scriptures, or any other book, never think *how* you read, but WHAT you read."—*Kemble.*

AFTER THE SERMON OR LESSON.

"He may not have lingually stumbled. His breaking down may not have been toward earth but toward heaven."
—*Dr. Parker.*

"Let them not put me off with admiration; its their salvation I want."—*Guthrie.*

CHANGED rather than
CHARMED.

IV. THE BIBLE AND CHILDHOOD.

(1.) **Man's Anxious Question about every child.** Luke i. 61.

(2.) *God's Interest in Childhood.* Gen. xxi. 17; Psa. cxlvii. 13; Prov. viii. 17.

(3.) **God's care for His Little Ones.** Deut. vii. 4; Psa. ciii. 13; Isiah xl. 11; Mal. iii. 7; Matt. vii. 11.

(4.) **God saving men by homefuls.** Gen. vii. 1; xix. 16; Josh. xxiv. 15; Acts xvi. 31–33.

(5.) **Parents as God-appointed teachers.** Deut. vi. 4–7; Psa. lxxviii. 5–7.

(6.) **Children to be early saved.** Matt. xix. 41; 2 Chron. xxxiv. 3; 1 Sam. iii. 1, 19.

---

1. THE BIBLE'S ESTIMATE OF CHILDHOOD.*

BY REV. W. F. CRAFTS.

In the very texture of some kinds of writing paper, as you hold it up to the light, you can see letters that were evidently stamped there during its manufacture. These are called the "water mark;" it is made while the paper is in a liquid state, and it constitutes the "trade mark" of the envelope. Metallic and glass articles also, in many cases, have trade marks wrought into their very substance while they are being made.

So, **every age has its trade mark**, unconsciously stamped upon it while its years are passing.

Geologists have discovered and classified these trade marks

---

* The religious, moral and educational questions connected with childhood are discussed at length in Mr. Craft's book, "Childhood, the Text-Book of the Age," which also contains six hundred incidents, both amusing and instructive, from child-life and child-thought, scientifically arranged in a "C__ __st __nd "Childhood's Dictionary," published by Lee & Shepard, Boston, Mass. Price $1.50.

in the case of the early ages, with scientific thoroughness. The Silurian age left its trade mark in fossil molluscs, the Devonian in fishes, the Carboniferous in coal plants, and the Triassic, with the feet of its monsters, put its eternal stamp into the sand and clay.

It is equally true that every historic age leaves its trade mark. A thorough archæologist and historian might arrange a cabinet of relics from the historic.

When the glaciers of geologic days, as giant sculptors, with whole continents as the blocks on which they were to work, carved out our mountains and valleys, they marked a period no more surely than the paintings and sculpture of Michael Angelo's day tell us of an age of refined and cultured leisure in history.

The "chromos," by which the works of the masters are now multiplied by the hundred thousand, will, perhaps, be the trade mark of our age in this line, indicating the reign of machinery and haste.

But the deepest and most striking trade-mark of our age is the recognition of the IMPORTANCE OF CHILDHOOD.

Never before did the world hear of so many children's picnics, and children's parties, and children's concerts, and juvenile books and magazines, and children's columns in all our papers, and "Children's Sermons," and "Children's Sundays" in our churches.

Men only a little past middle life can remember when there were not half-a-dozen children's books that had any extended circulation. To-day, a collection of the popular juvenile books would make the largest library in the world. Amid the multitudes of characters that Swift, and Field, and Defoe, and Scott gave to the world in their romances, scarce a little face appears. To-day no names of fiction are more familiar than "Little Paul," and "Little Nell," and "Tiny Tim," and "Eva" of "Uncle Tom's Cabin."

All this recognition of the rights and importance of childhood is but the starlight that shines upon us from above the manger of the God-child. It was Bethlehem that taught wise men that a child's face was a grander study than the stars.

The condition of childhood, then, is one of the best **thermometers** of the progress of an age or nation, and a sure test whether of the narrow or of the full development of Christianity in its midst.

Read the **sacred books** of India, China, Egypt, Persia, Greece and Rome, and you find hardly an indication that there are children in existence.

Turn to the Bible and you find it full of child-life and child-teaching.

Look at the **histories** outside of Palestine during Bible times—Berosus and Herodotus and Xenophon—and childhood's deeds and influence are scarcely mentioned.

Open to the historic parts of the Bible. The life of two lowly shepherd boys is given almost from their cradles until, at length, one becomes lord of Egypt, and the other the singing king of Israel. A little outcast child of slavery, a " foundling" from the flags of the Nile, has even his baby history carefully written, and the onward steps of his life, until he becomes the lawgiver of three millions of people.

A little maid is the heroine of a general's restoration from leprosy ; a little lad is the means of a great multitude being fed. We are told of the early strength of Sampson, the child-priesthood of Samuel, and the early Bible study of Timothy, who could know the Scriptures even in childhood, and by them be made wise unto salvation.

Three children are saved from death, or the point of death, by our Saviour, and the miracles are as faithfully described as those performed upon adults. No incidents in all the Bible are more beautifully noticed than the laying of Christ's hands upon the children's heads, and His expressed approval of their hosannas in the temple. Most wonderful of all, the Divine became a child to teach us that a child may become almost divine. The Germans have a beautiful legend that on Christmas morning the Child that was born in a manger revisits the earth to look after all the other little ones : that from the little prince in his royal cradle, to the baby sleeping like Himself in straw, none are left unvisited.

The legend is but another form of the truth that Bethlehem has brought Christ for ever near to the child-heart.

Look also into the **poetry** of Bible times outside of Palestine. In Homer and Virgil where are the lines for or about the children? Few indeed.

Turn to David: "Come ye children, hearken unto me, I will teach you the fear of the Lord."

Open to Isaiah: "Unto us a child is born, unto us a son is given."

Read the excellent **ethics** of Confucius and Plato. Where are the maxims that Timothy might know "from a child?" Open the ethical parts of the Bible, and read, "I have written unto *you*, little children." Or listen to the representative sentence of Proverbs: "*Hear ye, children*, the instructions of a father."

The ethics of the Bible put a high estimate on childhood. "It is not the will of your Father in heaven that one of these little ones should perish." In Sparta and some of the Greek cities, in Rome, and in many savage tribes, it was, and in heathen lands it is still, a common custom to destroy small and unhealthy children as soon as they are born. Christianity that weighs the baby's soul as well as its body, has saved from such a fate Sir Isaac Newton, Goethe, Talleyrand, Akenside, Walter Scott, Kepler, Samuel Johnson, Lord Nelson, Sir Christopher Wren, James Watt, Wilberforce, John Howard, Washington Irving, and many others who could "think God's thoughts after Him."

The ethics of Christianity also startled the world with the new doctrine, that to develop the grandest manhood we must "become as little children."

If any other system of ethics had been searched for the model of manhood, it would have presented stoical firmness, bold indifference to circumstances, or some other rough, stern virtue as our model; but Christ took a little child in the fields at play, and set him in the midst of His disciples, and said, "Except ye become as little children ye can in nowise enter into the kingdom of heaven." The way up was to go down in gentleness and humility. The meek shall inherit the earth.

"Gentleness" is to "make us great," and heirs of God's kingdom.

These were truths born of the Gospel, and impossible utterances outside of it. The very title of "*Gentleman*," could not have been spoken as a mark of honour save through the influence of Christianity.

George MacDonald calls attention to the words of Christ spoken after placing the child in the midst of His disciples, "Whosoever receiveth this little child receiveth me, and whosoever receiveth me, receiveth Him that sent me." So, he says, pure childhood is a revelation of Christ, as Christ is the manifestation of God ; that is, the childlike is the Christlike, yea more, it is the Godlike.

Leaving Bible times for **more recent ages**, we still find that the recognition of childhood is the unerring thermometer of the progress of Christianity. One of the first fruits of the great Reformation was the establishment of catechetical schools for children, and wherever its giant tread was felt, the same result was seen. Careful examination shows that the "great awakening" in England in the time of the Wesleys was the moving impulse from which the **modern Sunday School** sprang. As Christianity has deepened its work, child-culture has been more fully recognised as a Christian duty ; until, instead of Robert Raikes's ragged school, with paid teachers and the Bible only studied incidentally in connection with the simplest principles of common education, we have already in our most advanced schools a half-day Bible service of pastor, church, and children together, united by the bond of one topic, one text, one lesson—not only with each other, but also with the nation, with Canada, with England, with India, and ere long with all the Christian world.

Next to the Sunday-school, the grandest modern result of our Christianity in regard to the young is the discovery of that new world, the child-soul in its real feeling, characteristics, and wants, by the Columbus of modern education, Frederick Froebel, the originator of the **Kindergarten** method of developing childhood's powers.

The motto of this work is the motto of this age, "*Come, let us live for our children.*"

2. How shall we Manage Unruly Boys in the Sunday School?*

BY M. C. HAZARD.

There are **two classes** of unruly children†—First, from an **exuberance of spirits**. Second, **vicious**. How manage? 1. Do **not stop all innocent mirth**. 2. **Who should have charge**. **Not a stupid man**, a consecrated man, but a sharp consecrated man. 3. A man **not easily discouraged**. 4. Have **patience**. 5. **Never give up**. 6. Really **love them**. 7. Take them **singly**.

THE SAME QUESTION ANSWERED BY CHARLES M. MORTON.

1st. Do **not expect too much** in taking a Sunday School class; do not be concerned that you shall be appreciated; you will be appreciated if worthy of it.

2nd. Give them **attention**; personal intercourse. Lay **responsibilities** upon them; give them something to do.

3rd. **Never be discouraged.**‡

---

3. "How can we get Young Pupils to Study their Lessons at Home?" §

BY MRS. W. F. CRAFTS.

Several facts in connection with this subject are too generally overlooked:

---

* 1 Thess. v. 14; Rev. ii. 5; Jas. i. 5.

† In opening Mr. Hazard said, that his first experience on this question came through an attempt to manage a class of unruly girls. In nearly every class there would be found some unruly scholars. He then described an ideal boy—one having snap, with a ring in his voice, fire in his eye, and an appetite perfectly appalling.

‡ Illustrated by seven years of labor for three boys in Mission School of Plymouth Church.

§ Nearly every point in this article would be as appropriate to classes of adults as to classes of young people.

(1.) By far the largest proportion of young people, even those almost grown to maturity have **no commentaries or lesson periodicals in their houses.** If teachers with their superior advantages of experience and study and Christian zeal, need lesson helps and a meeting for mutual study in order to be prepared on the lessons, how can we expect any considerable preparation on a new lesson by scholars who have only the lesson leaf or question book? This difficulty might be partially obviated however, by introducing the "Scholar's Quarterly" published at the office of *The Sunday School Times* in Philadelphia, or "The Scholar's Hand Book" published at the office of the *Sunday School World* in the same city, or by inducing scholars to subscribe for the low-priced monthlies, *The International Lesson Monthly* of Chicago, or *The Sunday School Journal* of New York, each costing in clubs only 60 cents a year. For some time at least, in most of our schools, it will, however, remain true that most of our scholars have no such lesson helps as they need for proper preparation.

(2.) It is also true that **most young people do not feel any special interest** in a new lesson from the Bible, and as there can be no real compulsion in Sunday School teaching as in secular teaching, increased study at home must be secured by rousing an increased mental and moral interest in the work to be done, not by any arbitrary rules. In every class, some at least will lack this needed interest in lesson study.

Accepting these two facts, the lack of helps, and the lack of interest, how can we secure more home study of the lessons? This hardest of all the hard questions of the Sunday School I think may be answered from a standard practice of Normal School Teachers. When thus engaged in teaching geography to a class of children, I always talked over the lesson with the class before it was given them to study, explaining, illustrating, vivifying the topic, and then sending the little pupils to their seats or to their homes with this awakened interest to write down all they could remember of what I had said, and then to take their books and after that memorize the words of the text-book which had already been explained.

This principle, applied to the Sunday School, would lead the teacher whose scholars do not study at home to the following method of teaching :—

(1.) By explanations, suggestions and questions, **to rouse an interest in the lesson of the day**, and to show how and when to study it out, spending at least one-third of the time allowed for lesson study in rousing this interest.

(2.) To ask the memorizing of the Golden Text, or parts of the lesson, **after**, rather than *before* **the rousing of this interest.**

(3.) To **make much of reviewing**, recalling what has been told in a lesson, at its close (whether there is a public review or not); asking parents to review it regularly at home also; asking scholars to tell at home all they can remember, or to write it out and bring it the next Sunday; recalling it yet again after a week has passed at the beginning of the next lesson study; reviewing still farther at the end of each month, each quarter, and each year. No one who understands the human mind, or the principles of education will say that this is "making too much of reviewing."

(4.) **This method would be carried out in detail in about this way :** (*a*) **Before the study of the lesson** in the classes, the superintendent or pastor makes a three or five minutes review of the lesson of the preceding Sabbath, asking for repetition of its Golden Text and memory verses. (*b*) **At the beginning of class study** teacher spends at least one-third of the time allotted for the class work in questioning back, more in detail, this previous lesson, and also in questioning it into the minds of the class more fully, and more correctly, asking for additional knowledge which pupils have been able to find, and illustrating, adapting and enforcing this lesson. (*c*) **The teacher uses the latter portion of the time** allowed to class work, one half or two thirds to opening up the lesson for the day, rousing curiosity, and pointing out features of interest and methods of studying it, spending two or three minutes at the end in *questioning back* and *questioning in* all she has told or developed in regard to this new lesson. (*d*) The pastor or superintendent also makes **a brief, public review of this new lesson** in such a way as to send the school home with an interest to study it still farther and memorize the appointed parts. (*e*) The lesson is **then read** responsively **in the closing** instead of the *opening* **exercises**, after it has been clothed with meaning and interest. (*f*) At the close of the session, teacher charges the class to **talk the lesson** over **at home**, "tell mother," or write out all they can remember and bring it back the next week, and also to commit to memory the passages in the lesson just opened that are appointed for memorizing, which have now an interest and relish about them. (*g*) **Parents question back the new lesson** at home.

In this way a teacher may be saved from the apparent necessity of lecturing to unprepared, unanswering and uninterested pupils, and more study, more interest, and more memorizing of Scripture may be secured. It will be seen that this method neither necessitates nor precludes the study of the new lesson before coming to the class.

---

4. "How Can we Secure a More General Attendance of Children at Preaching Services?"

AN INSTITUTE CONVERSATION.

1. Invite them publicly and personally.
2. Simplify preaching.
3. Superintendent should call attention of school to the preaching service. Announce and urge attendance.
4. Give children something to do in connection with the service.
5. Review sermon in Sunday School.

6. Parents should require their children to attend preaching.*
7. Pastors should notice children in their pastoral calls.
8. Preaching on subject of lesson after study by the school.
9. Teachers inviting pupils to their pews.
10. Have comfortable pews.
11. Have episodes in the sermons for the children.
12. Parents should attend Sunday School and respect it as one of the services of the church.†
13. Children's sermons occasionally at least.
14. Prayers shorter, hymns and tunes brighter.
15. As early rising on Sunday morning as on other days of the week.

---

* DR. VINCENT sent forth a timely article not long since in the *Christian Advocate*, on the "Absence of Children from the Preaching Service." In it he says:—

The principal fault lies with parents themselves. There is too little home discipline of any sort nowadays. A child who does not want to go to church is permitted to stay at home without any good reason. He "does not want to go," he "does not see the use," he "will not go." And so parents allow their children to do as they please. Not, indeed, in reference to the public school are they permitted to choose for themselves. To that they must go, whether they wish to or not. And so they go. Parents are not afraid to prejudice their children in regard to secular studies, but when the attendance at preaching is in question there is no parental authority; or, at least, there is the largest degree of laxity. Now, I assert that *parents are responsible for the absence of the children from the pews on Sunday morning.* Let a man resolve that his family shall be at church, and they will be there. My father, an active worker in the church—trustee, class-leader, superintendent—always took his children with him. They never thought of neglecting any one of the church services with which they were connected.

It is not merely authority that is needed at home, but an appeal to the child's conscience. Let a boy express disinclination to attend service; show him that he owes all that he has to his heavenly Father; show him the propriety of keeping up the public recognition of God; show him the divine commands which call us to the house of God. In ninety-nine cases out of one hundred the boy will see the duty in a clear light, and his conscience will take him to the sanctuary.

† A pastor sends out the following on a postal card to the adults of his congregation:—

You are cordially invited by your pastor to be present next Sunday at 10.30 A.M., in our church Bible Service, when we hope to honor our Divine Lord by obeying his command to "Search the Scriptures." John v. 39. How should we do this? Read Prov. ii. 4, 5. "If thou seekest her as silver, and searchest for her as for hid treasures; then shalt thou understand the fear of the Lord, and find the knowledge of God." The Scripture lesson for to-day is Proverbs i. 20-33.

THE CALL OF WISDOM.

There will be several adult classes in charge of competent teachers, and you will not be called upon individually to answer any question. If you can not be with us during the entire service will you not come at 11.30 A.M., to listen to a Black Board Sermon by the Pastor?

Services as usual afternoon and evening.

Your loving Pastor,
S. L. GRACEY.

5. Preaching to Children.*

By Rev. Richard Newton, D.D.

I suppose you have all seen *an india-rubber face?* And I dare say you have amused yourself by pinching it one way and pulling it another, and seeing what different expressions it will put on. But when you stop pulling or pinching it, it returns to the same face that it was before.

Now your faces are softer than india-rubber, and they are full of little strings called muscles. These muscles, or strings, are pulled one way, or pulled another, just according to your feelings. Sometimes you feel grieved or sad, and the little muscles pull your face into a very doleful expression. The moment anybody looks at you they know something is troubling you, and you feel sorrowful. But if you see a funny picture, or if something happens to make you feel merry and glad, the little muscles pull your face into smiles and dimples, and you look just ready to burst out into a broad laugh.

But when we commit sin, wicked feelings are at work pulling these strings. Anger pulls one set of strings, and then you know what a disagreeable look the face puts on in a moment! Pride pulls another set of these strings, and so does vanity, or envy, or deceit, or discontent; and each of these brings its own peculiar look or expression over the face. And the worst thing about it is, that if these strings are pulled too often the face will not return to what it was before; but the strings will become stiff, like wires, and the face will keep wearing the ugly look it put on all the time. By giving way to sin, or indulging their bad feelings, some people get their faces worked up to such a dreadful look that, when you meet one of them in the street, the moment you see him you can tell what his character is,

A face that was very lovely when it was that of a child, if it has the passion of anger often pulling at it, will get at last to wear all the time a sullen, cross, dissatisfied look. Or, if a

---

*Dr. Newton is known the world over as the greatest of preachers to children, and every teacher of the young, whether in the pulpit or Sunday School, ought to read at least a few of his many volumes of Sermons to Children. Published by Carter Brothers, New York.

man has learned to love money better than anything else, and to hoard it up for its own sake, this will pull a set of strings that will fix a close, mean, grasping look upon his face, so that as you pass him you will be ready to say, "There goes a miser!" Or, if any one learns to lie and steal, his face will show it by and by; it will be impossible for him to put on an honest, truthful look.

You know, my dear children, the Bible tells us that sin is a reproach, or a disgrace, and if we consent to it, or give way to it, it will pull those strings in our faces that will make our very looks to be disgraceful. Don't let anger, or pride, or passion get hold of the strings, or they will make you appear so ugly that no one will love to look at you. But let love, and gentleness, and good-will, and truth, and honesty have hold of the strings, and they will make your faces beautiful and lovely.

We are able to give only the closing part of Dr. Newton's Sermon on THE **P**OWER **P**LEASURE **P**ROFIT OF GENTLENESS.

---

6. THE LESSON IN THE PRIMARY CLASS.

BY MRS. W. F. CRAFTS.

The International Lesson is adapted to the Primary Classes. Every Sunday School Periodical of the day contains a special adaptation of it for this class. It is the aim of the Lesson Committee to select such topics as may be suitable for "little children, young men, and teachers." They have been successful, and an experience of five years in writing and teaching the International Lesson to little people proves its practicability.

"**Chirp Right**" is Dr. Ormiston's advice to the infant-class teacher—a wise bit of advice drawn from his experience as a boy in trying to feed callow young birds in imitation of the mother-bird.

Fully Prepared a teacher should be, and perfectly independent of notes or question book. "A fixed purpose and an emancipated eye" is Dr. Vincent's rule for the teacher.

Seek to make one definite point rather than try to teach the entire lesson. Select the aspect of the lesson that most fully meets the condition of the individual members of the class.

Make the lesson contribute to the child's love of the Bible. Let the teacher frequently open the Bible and reverently read from it at impressive points in the lessons.

---

7. THE LESSON IN THE PRIMARY CLASS.

BY MISS JENNY B. MERRILL.

1. It is very **seldom advisable to use all** the selected verses.

2. It is necessary to **study the context** and parallel passages.

3. The **introduction** should be carefully selected. It should be short, leading to the lesson. A good introduction is like a wedge, opening the mind for the reception of the lesson.

(1.) If in the lesson **some familiar scene**, object or action is suggested, it will prove **a good starting point.**

(2.) The **Golden Text** when very simple may be used **as an introduction.** Example—"She hath done what she could," asking: "Who can it be? I wonder what she did?" &c.

(3.) **A picture containing a scene of the lesson** may be presented; the children, telling all they see in it, are led to wonder what it means.

(4.) The Golden Text may **be developed** by familiar illustrations, and the children afterward led to discover that the lesson of the day is also an illustration of the Golden Text.

(5.) **Many questions** should be asked; descriptions should be minute; development work should be much used. When the lesson consists of general statements use illustrations from which the general statement may be drawn. Example: Prov. i. 25—illustration, Noah.

(6.) It is very helpful to use **illustrations that reach the eye**. The objects should be put out of sight as soon as they have done their work. The following objects have served this purpose:—Flowers, blocks, seeds, wheat, silver, gold, brass, iron, &c.

(7.) Very often the children may be allowed to do **some little act with their hands** during the lesson, as making a letter, figure or line on blackboard; making a letter with their fingers (of the deaf and dumb alphabet). They may place their two hands together and hold them like a book and "make believe" read. One child may show the class some action, as laying in the Oriental position at a table, etc. These little acts are centres of attraction that exert their influence for some distance in the lesson.

(8.) The **lesson should be made practical and personal**. Often, a little gift may be given as a remembrance of the lesson, that it may be recalled during the week and so associated with their daily life. Something may be suggested for the children to do during the week in accordance with the teaching of the lesson, and the next Sabbath the teacher should not forget to inquire about it.

---

8. The Conversion of Children.

BY MRS. W. F. CRAFTS.

"**As early in a child's life as possible**, teach him implicit trust in Christ, and the full consecration of his little life, with all its possibilities, to Christ."* Jesus is willing to re-

---

* Dr. Vincent.

ceive them, for He has said "Suffer the little ones to come unto me." The cold world and the cold church utter in a different voice, "They are too young to learn Truth," but let the teacher who has faith in child piety also have faith in God's blessing on the work of leading these little ones to Him.

The smallest child can love Him for His love. The teacher should try to realize something of the value of a child's soul by considering the ransom price paid for it—even the blood of the only begotten Son of God. Little children realize their duty to God better than their elders comprehend it for them. A company of children were asked, "How old do you think children ought to be before they begin to pray?" "As soon as they can speak, as soon as they can understand," "One year old," were the replies. "How old do you think children ought to be before they begin to pray in prayer meeting?" was next asked. "Five," "six," "ten," "twelve," were the respective answers. No one said, Not until they are grown up. "How long have you been a Christian?" a boy was asked who had made a prayer in the meeting. "Ever since I can remember," was spoken with a glowing face. The child Christian cannot be like the adult Christian. It is as praiseworthy to play like a Christian as it is to trade like a Christian.

"I am never satisfied to teach a lesson without bringing Christ into it," was the remark of an earnest primary teacher. Surely

"All growing that is not towards God
Is growing to decay."

Let every lesson, then, have Christ in it.

There should be a weekly class prayer-meeting. Children should be taught to pray with the heart and with the understanding. Lip service in any form is not pleasing to God.

Children should be taught to pray both morning and evening in their homes. Habits of prayer in childhood make it easier in after life to keep up regular prayer.

Personal conversation on religion should enter into every teacher's work. This should be done, if possible, with the co-operation of parents.

Covenant for Young Christians.*

THE CHILDREN'S CHRISTIAN BAND.

> "MY LAMBS." | "SEEK ME EARLY."
>
> Dear Little Friend,
>
> Can you, from your heart, answer "yes" to the following questions :—
>
> Do you love Jesus?
>
> Are you trusting in Jesus as your own precious Saviour?
>
> Will you try, by the help of Jesus, to give up everything that is sinful?
>
> Will you try to be more like Jesus every day?

Name,.. Residence,..

The Conversion of Children.

By Rev. J. E. Latimer, D.D.

I. The **scriptural argument** regarding the condition of children.

This clusters around three definite passages of Scripture, viz.: The authorities between Adam and Christ, in the 5th of Romans; the utterance of Christ when He declares that children belong to the Kingdom of Heaven; and the passage "their angels do always behold the face of our Father in Heaven."

---

* Used by the Children's Christian Band, Surrey Chapel, London.

II. The Theological argument.

This is a statement of the position held generally by the Christian Church.

The child is born a sinner, constructively at least, and this is not by his own fault, rather his misfortune. The atoning work of Christ provides for him and saves him.

Meyer thinks that only those who have the child-like spirit are intended, and only adults. The true view is, that all infant children are included, and all like them in spirit. Can we predicate regeneration of the child? This is variously answered.

Dr. Nast and Bishop Merrill say no. Dr. Hibbard only says that it is in the child what regeneration is in the adult.

Dr. Fisk seconds Fletcher in saying that adult sinners have sinned away the justification of infants.

Dr. Whedon holds that adult sinners are apostates from the grace of infancy.

Pro. Hedge asserts that infants are saved, and claims this to have been always the position of Calvinists.

Dr. Hodge in his systematic theology teaches the same. These two positions have significance in that they show how we enter upon our probation.

III. The practical argument.

Education should begin with the first breath of the child. The first and almost only duty of the Christian mother is to culture her child for Christ.

There are two methods of education—the objective and subjective. True education will combine them both. The mother's instinct and the grace of God will lead her to the accomplishment of these results, though she may never have heard of any of the methods of the books and theorists. From the point where the child comes to conscious personality, which is back of the point of memory, the child may turn to Christ. This is the time for a mother to work. The child born in a

Christless home starts from the same platform, but has not the same culture to develop this inward grace.—The child of Christian parents has everything in his favor except his evil heart. But some object that the children of Christian parents do not meet the demands of this theory. The difficulty is often that they are only half Christians and have no right to claim the promises. But how is it of earnest, faithful, Christian parents? There must be some misapprehension of their privilege, or some vice in their method. The laws of moral government and the promises of God are not uncertain, but as sure as gravity.

IV. The economic argument.

The church works at a disadvantage in that it waits for the child to be swept away from Christ and then strives to conquer them back. Is it not time that we should begin to train up in Christ, and increase the church rather by training than by revival? More than this, the church receives a great loss in the loss of childhood experience, which is peculiar as in woman.

V. Function of the Sunday School.

It is the work of the Sunday School to apply these forces to the childhood mind. More than ever, the Sunday School is to be the nursery of the church. Especially has it a work for the children of unconverted parents.

The Christian Culture of Converted Children.

By Rev. John H. Castle, D.D.

Cant. vii. 12; John xxi. 15; Eph. iv. 13.

Except when some great tide of revival is rolling through the land, the vast majority of the accessions to all our churches are children and youths. When children are converted, what then? The common practice is to leave the converts to themselves. Not a tithe as much interest is taken in them after their conversion as before—as though the great end had been secured.

But have you noticed that the whole of the New Testament is addressed to converts, and not the impenitent and unbelieving? The Epistles are almost exclusively occupied with the culture of converts.—"Culture" suggests the growth of plants; not in the wild wood or unbroken moor or prairie, but in a garden under the oversight and skill of the experienced gardener.

1. The plant. It must be **one of God's own plants**.

2. For God's own Plants He has provided **a garden, the church**.

3. A wise gardener will be much more concerned at the beginning about the development of **roots** than of leaves, branches and blossoms. The soil in which to root a young convert is the truth of God's word.

4. The convert-culturist will, like the gardener, jealously watch the appearance of **weeds**.

Two kinds of seed, bad and good.

The richer the soil the more prolific the weeds.

If you would save yourself the trouble and toil of weeding out, keep the soil thoroughly occupied with good seed.

5. Not only will the gardener strive to keep his ground free from weeds, but will often **prune** his plants and vines.

Isa. xviii. 5: "For afore the harvest, when the bud is perfect, and the sour grape is ripening in the flower, he shall both cut off the sprigs with pruning hooks, and take away and cut down the branches."

6. All the labor is in order to the production of **fruit** of the best quality, and in the greatest abundance.

It may now be worth our while to consider some of the fruits we should aim to produce in convert-culture.

(*a*) **Fulness and force of personal character.** A man is greater than his work and worth more.

(*b*) A modest but hearty and fearless **confession of Christ.**

(*c*) Power and tact in the **resistance of temptation.**

(*d*) **Activity** in some branch of church work.

(*e*) A larger spirit of **pecuniary sacrifice** to the cause of Christ than has hitherto prevailed among Christians.

(*f*) A taste not only for the **word of God,** but for general **Christian knowledge** and information.

(*g*) **Symmetry** of Christian character.

At this point allow me to suggest a few cautions:

1. Be careful to cultivate in the direction of **natural traits,** otherwise you may destroy individuality of character and capacity. All must not, therefore, be subject to the same culture.

2. **Avoid cant.** Cultivate naturalness in expression.

3. There is a possibility of **too much culture,** or rather too much cultivating. Two extremes—entire neglect and over-culture. A little wholesome neglect would be desirable in some families.

4. Do not forget that God is ever carrying forward His own peculiar cultivation of converts; "Ye are **God's husbandry.**"

To whom are we to look to do this work of Christian training?

1. To Christian **parents.**
2. To the **pastors** of our churches.

And yet it will not do for the church to cast all on the pastor. He is the engineer who controls the great Corliss engine of the church; but it is too much to expect that the engineer shall watch and guide every machine which is set in motion in the church.

3. **Church officers.**
4. Sunday School **teachers.** These have special facilities.
5. All **mature Christians**—the church of the future.

9. Christian Home Culture.

BY REV. A. H. MUNRO.

It is questionable whether we shall be able to accomplish much more in connection with Sabbath School work than we are doing without a more perfect co-operation between the homes and the school. When these are both what they should be, they alternate the offices of Paul and Apollos; each sows for the other to water, and each waters what the other sows, and God gives the increase. What do Christian parents require to give their families the home culture they should receive?

1. A deep abiding conviction that **the duty is one God has laid upon them**, and which they can neither neglect nor delegate to others with impunity.

2. **A definite purpose** in relation to its performance. The Christian parent should have a clear conception of what he is to aim at in the religious culture of his children, and his object should not be to raise them up to the level of worldly respectability or the average of religious profession, but to make them the sons and daughters of the Lord Almighty, and consistent followers of Christ.

3. **Character.** It is power, and nowhere more so than in the family. The choice, too, that is needed to guide and influence the family life aright, is that of the renewed heart and meek-loving spirit in communion with God. But in addition to these qualifications the Christian parent needs principles to guide him in the religious culture of his family.

Those principles should be few, comprehensive, infallible, and practical. Among them should be these :—

(1.) That in the pursuit of the object sought in Christian home culture, namely, the formation and development of Christian character, **God's grace must be the** dependence, His Word the authority, and His Son the example.

(2.) That **the whole nature**, body, intellect, and heart, is to be regarded and treated as a divine creation of which sin is the perversion and ruin, and godliness the true cultivation and blessed use.

(3.) That **the whole life is a unit**, which, without separation into secular and religious parts, should be made a free, holy, harmonious service unto God.

(4.) That **all true, good, and beautiful things belong to Christ**, and should be used by His people to elevate, adorn, and bless human life. Rules must be adopted based on these principles, but only to avert some evil or to secure some benefit, and often as much wisdom will be exhibited in the suspension of a rule as in its observance.

How many parents' hearts ache as they remember errors they have committed in the government of their families, producing effects they did not foresee and cannot remedy? Alas, we most of us get our wisdom too late.

We begin to know how to take care of our children when they cease to need our care and go from us to repeat, perhaps in a worse form, the errors we committed in relation to themselves. Is not something more than an occasional sermon or book needed to direct attention to this subject? If it is deemed wise and right to hold conventions, institutes, and classes for those who have the care of our children for one hour during the Sabbath, would it not be equally wise and right to do something similar in behalf of those who have the care of their children all the hours, of all the days, of all the years, from infancy to maturity? Why not have Parents' Institutes, to which parents and mothers could be invited, and to which they would come with tender hearts that would respond to every appeal, and hungry minds that would grasp at every suggestion made by able and earnest men, who would speak to them in relation to the varied and important elements of home culture? I advocate such institutes being established. We need, and can have them, and they will do incalculable good.

The people of this great country may well feel elated in this centennial year of their national history. But the wisest and most thoughtful are too patriotic to shut their eyes to portentous facts which tell too plainly that, however excellent the public and Sabbath schools of this land, a great and extended improvement is needed in Christian home culture to avert evils that threaten, and to make this highly-favored country all that God has made possible for it to be.

---

0. THE SUNDAY SCHOOL AND THE HOME.

BY HENRY WARD BEECHER.

The best Sabbath School is but a poor substitute for the family. The foundation institution of time and the world is the household, and although the household depends upon the nature of civil constitutions and laws, upon the influences which are derived from the church and from schools, yet Governments and Churches and Schools are themselves more dependent upon the family than the family is upon them. There is nothing which can save a nation whose sills are rotted out; a nation may be cut off utterly in all its growth and development, but if the household, which is its foundation, remains intact and pure, it will spring up again in spite of all adversity.

When Napoleon the First overran Germany he reduced that nation almost to bankruptcy and despair. Then it was that Steine, the great forecasting statesman, advised his King wisely that the hope of that Empire lay in the more absolute and thorough education of the household, and that was in modern times the origin upon any large scale of free, common education among the people. From out of that state of depression Germany sprang to be, as she is to-day, the tallest Protestant nation in Europe; and France, that ground her to powder, has seen the change by which she is under, and Germany super-eminent. And the change has been wrought out through the education of the children.

I have said that the best Sabbath School is but a poor substitute for the family school, for no Sabbath School can do more than teach. To be sure example goes a certain way, but that itself is part and parcel of teaching. The command is not anywhere, nor is the promise anywhere, teach a child the way he should go and when he is old he will not depart from it; the declaration is, train a child in the way he should go, and when he is old he will not depart from it. It is teaching reduced to habits—that is training, and we are to train children; but there is no institution comparable to the household for that, because it teaches them earlier than anything else can. But it is chiefly so because there more than anywhere else love is the teacher, and it is the wisdom and power of love which enforces the lesson; the teaching, moreover, is not given only one day in seven to a class of six or eight altogether, and is not through the ministration of words alone, but it is given with the eye, the gentle hand, and mother's touch, day and night suffering for and with her children, and helping them at the point of time when temptation assails them.

So in many ways family teaching is the nearest approach to Divine moral government that the world has ever known, or probably ever will know, for there is no legislature, no administration, no philosophical teaching that can for a single moment do the things which centralized love, born of God and ministered by the Divine Spirit, can do in the education and full development of human nature.

Now, the principal danger we are under in pressing forward this great economy of our day—the Sunday School as the university for children—is that we shall supersede the family, that the father and mother will remit to the school the duty of instructing the children. Happily, however, they cannot remit to it the duty of discipline. The household still will be a training institution, but more and more the effects of the Sabbath School will be to cause less attention to be given in some households to the instruction of the children, and this danger is so great that, if it were not for other reasons, I think it might be a very serious question whether we were not more in danger of losing, on the whole, by Sabbath Schools if they weakened the duties of the family, more than we should gain by them. But when we consider how many children have no parents, and how many are without parents fit to teach, how the majority of every community is without any such opportunity, there is no doubt as to the wisdom of having Sabbath Schools.

Now, receiving the children into our hands in Sabbath Schools, is there any scriptural way more than another by which we may hope to raise up a generation to serve God? Is human nature for ever to be that thing we know it to be now? Is weakness, with occasional strength, for ever to characterise Christian communities? Are there to be no discoveries in religion that will measure themselves against the discoveries in science?

As men are learning a better agriculture, better mechanical arts, better administrations; as nations are learning to be better nations, and international arbitration is becoming more general, are we to expect nothing better on the side of religion? For mere geographic spread of religion is not growth, mere extension is not development. We may spread the Gospel till there shall be no place without a Bible, and yet religion may not have been developed.

Religion is the development of larger power in the souls of men; it is by the growth of the fruit of the Spirit planted in the better soil we are to expect the advent of that religious power which we believe is yet one day to come before the second appearing of the Lord.

Is there, then, any way in which we can do better than we have done? Is there to be no further development of Christian power than in the days gone by? I think there is to be. It is to this point I wish to direct my remarks, viz.: that it is the duty of ministers, church officers, and all teachers and scholars to make religion more attractive and more beautiful to man than it has yet been made.

We must show the world that religion is the true nature, that man's first nature is his spiritual nature, and that the underground nature is his own work. It is true that in our lower or animal nature we are depraved. Man has a double being—that of the soul and that of the body—which are constantly struggling with each other, sometimes the one uppermost, sometimes the other. Man is born an animal, and a very poor one too.

Nothing is so small, nothing so absolutely negative, as the most glorious thing God ever created—a man. An insect is as perfect five minutes after it is born as five days afterwards. Not so with a child, which is a mere compound-suction animal, and lies in the arms of its mother helpless, nearer to zero than anything else. So the child grows up, but through months and years remains quite incapable of culture. Not till after one year does it begin to discern things, and not then the distinction between right and wrong. So little by little the child learns to help itself, to run and fight and do all those things which nature requires of animals. It is not till somewhat later that the affections develop in any marked degree, and the time at which moral sense is developed differs with different children.

So we have man as an animal first, and afterwards the development of his moral sentiments. The question is this. Are we to teach and preach a system of administration and of means which is adapted to animal man, and never overtop it by a system which will be adapted to spiritual man? The animal man must be governed very much as is an ox or an ass. First, he must find by physical coercion that he must obey, and that is the beginning of God to any animal: he cannot help it, and therefore he obeys. It is not from preference, but in order to avoid something worse. The lower conditions of savage life and of life in the household are, and must continue to be, an adaptation of means to ends according to the circumstances of the creature which is being taught.

A great many parents don't believe in physical discipline, in rigorous government, for the little animal child. They say, "govern the child by reason." What! govern the child by reason before there is any? "Well," they say, "govern a child by gentleness and patience." If a woman is placed in a good position, inheriting virtues from her parents, with a mind well balanced and cultured, married happily and placed in circumstances of ease, and has three children, I can well understand how she can have patience to bring them up anyhow.

But take a poor washerwoman who has sixteen children, and tell her to bring up her fiery little cub by moral suasion, and she will reply that it is impossible. There is no way of bringing up children except according to their conditions. The economic method is, that while the child is in the animal condition, you should address it with animal influences. But the object is not to control the child by a physical discipline because it was the best. It was the lowest method, and was practicable only because the child is in such a low condition he cannot be taught any other way. As quickly as possible the child should be taught by a higher method. To tell a child, " You shall go to bed without your supper," is a very good punishment for a child up to a certain age; but " You shall go to bed without your kiss" is better, and " You shall go to bed because you have grieved your Father which is in Heaven " is better still, but it comes later in life.

Has not the Christian Church and the community come to that condition in which Sabbath Schools and congregations can be appealed to by the higher and grander influences of Christianity than by the lower? Is it not time for men to begin to understand the power and attractions of the beauty of holiness?

There is nothing so beautiful on earth in development as a true Christian spirit working in the actual affairs of human life, and nothing in the Heavens so beautiful as God. If we could see Him all light would die from the sun and all blossoms would wither from the earth, for He is the chief among ten thousand and altogether lovely. Weary heart, strive and struggle for a little while, for there is not a hand's-breadth between Heaven and some of you, and for the first time in your life you will be able to say " I am satisfied," when you behold God and rejoice in His beauty. When I look into the Bible and read the lives of the Apostles and disciples, I find myself in company with a very different set of men from the average of men in our churches. I find none more noble and courteous than Paul, or who stood more for his rights, and yet none more gentle and more perfectly self-sacrificing. It was not, however, a raw-boned, hard-featured self sacrifice that makes you feel sorry he does it, but that triumphant and truly Christian self-sacrifice that makes itself beautiful.

Paul and all his compatriots were singing men in their adversity, trials, and troubles. When in prison, the hymns and prayers of Paul and Silas were mightier than stone or iron. If men would meet adversity and trouble with prayer and rejoicing, human sorrow would have less dominion over them. When

Paul said, "Ye are the temples of the Holy Ghost," he presented to the mind of the Jews the grand white marble temple at Jerusalem, which is still the glory of that old race, than which there is not to-day a better stock. I have been thoroughly indignant often by the way in which men are appealed to on the subject of religion. They are told that if they don't repent they will go to hell.

It is very true, and some people should be told it. Men often open the door of the church as if it were a grave's door, and say, "There is the church and there is hell—take your choice!" They say, "Well, if that is the choice, on the whole we would rather—well, we don't know." The preacher then flashes lightnings at them, and when they have reached middle life, and pretty much all of youth and pleasure has fled, they conclude to crawl in. What is their idea of religion under such circumstances? Instead of fishing and hunting they say they will keep the Sabbath they will not swear, except under an immense pressure of temptation; they will read the Bible every day, if they don't forget it, but on Sunday anyhow. They will pay their proportion (they being the judges what that is) towards the support of Gospel ordinances, and they don't know exactly about the outcome, and they prefer to give in their belief in creeds wholesale. When I see hard tobacco-chewing Christian men leaving the Bible out of their religion and hoping a good deal in the goodness of God, I am sad.

The substance of religion, as described by the Apostle Paul, is that every man shall be responsible for his own acts. The majority of men are not led to accept the truth of religion on account of the arguments made in its behalf, but by the personal life of Christians. If you look at those men who are most truly Christians you will find they are as free as the birds —they are the children of God. Sabbath School teachers should teach the children that in accepting Christ they become glorious and free. Teachers cannot teach what is a religious life by words alone, they must live it. Some Christians are like fire-flies at night, they fly in the darkness and flash, and none are able to steer by them. Some, on the other hand, are like the lighthouse on these islands; they stand during summer and winter, day and night, showing forth a steady, bright light, so that every pilot that goes from this mighty river knows how to steer his ship. "Let your light so shine before men that they knowing your good works may glorify your Father who art in Heaven."

V. THE BIBLE AND SUNDAY SCHOOL MACHINERY

(1) **Importance of Orderly Arrangement.** 1 Cor. xiv. 40, 33.

(2) **Officers and Division of Labor.** 1 Cor. xii. 28; 1 Kings iv. 1-7.

(3) **Financial Arrangements.** Neh. x. 32; 1 Cor. xvi. 2.

(4) **Illustrative Helps.** Matt. xiii. 34.

(5) **Sacred Music.** 1 Chron. xv. 22; Neh. xii. 46; 2 Chron. xxix. 25-31.

(6) **Sunday School Exercises.** Colos. iii. 16.

(7) **Spirituality Pervading All.** 1 Cor. xiii. 1; Ezek. i. 20; 1 Cor. xiv. 15.

1. Names for the Sunday School.

It is called "**Bible Service**,"* "Sunday School," "Teaching Service," "Bible School," "Church School," "Children's Service."

---

*A test vote, at the Sunday School Parliament, as to the preferable name gave "Bible Service" the majority, the other names following in the order of the vote, the last name (used in Continental Europe) getting no vote at all.

The main *objection* to all names containing the word "School" is that the word "School," as commonly used, covers the two thoughts, *youth* and *education*, while the religious institution to which the word is applied is adapted to the *aged* as well as the *young*, and seeks the *salvation* even more than the *education* of its members.

The main argument in favor of names containing the word "service" is that it is the word used in speaking of "The Preaching Service," and thus puts the two, as they should be, on an equal footing of honor and work.

---

2. The Sunday School-Room and Library Plan.

Sunday School architecture could not be satisfactorily presented in the brief space that could be allowed in this volume, and we therefore refer those interested in this subject to illustrated representations of the subject, with engraved plans, in the "Normal Class" for March and November, 1875, and also in "The Ideal Sunday School," by Rev. W. F. Crafts; Henry Hoyt, 9 Cornhill, Publisher; in paper covers 25 cents. In "The Ideal Sunday School" a library plan is also given.

---

3. Sunday School Constitutions.

(1.) There should be **a full and explicit statement** of the duties of the pastor and the other officers and teachers of the Sunday School, thus preventing and correcting errors constitutionally rather than personally.*

---

* For instance, it would prevent much misunderstanding between pastors and superintendents, and correct many neglects of duty, if their relative duties were constitutionally defined and occasionally read. The best way also to tell the officers that they are not to be "interrupters" of the teachers during the lesson is to put such a clause among their specified duties in the constitution. That Superintendent who was asked by a correspondent to send him his Sunday School Constitution and replied, "I'm busy and can't come," was more witty than wise. The Sunday School ought not to be an absolute monarchy. So long as officers are human we shall need constitutions to prevent abuses and cultivate right methods in the Sunday School as well as the State.

(2.) The constitution should be **read** in the presence of officers and teachers at least once a quarter.

(3.) **Printed copies** should also be supplied to officers and teachers at least.

(4.) Only the officers, teachers and appointed representatives from the church should be allowed to vote in **the election of officers**—adult members of classes yielding this privilege because of the evils that would naturally result from allowing the whole Sunday School to participate in elections.

(5.) It should be stated in a Sunday School Constitution that **no one who is not a Christian** is eligible to the position of superintendent, assistant superintendent or teacher.*

---

4. Sunday School Programme.

(1.) Teachers' Prayer Meeting, with roll call of officers and teachers. (Twenty minutes.)

(2.) Teachers' Sociable. (Three minutes.)

(3.) Teachers in their places. (Seven minutes previous to opening.)

(4.) Class Sociables. (Five minutes.)

(5.) Organ Voluntary. (Instead of Opening Bell.

(6.) Greeting by Superintendent.

(7.) Brief Prayer. (Silent prayer, or Lord's Prayer.

(8.) Song.

---

* We should as soon send our children to sea, with a captain and crew utterly ignorant of the laws of navigation, as send them to be instructed in eternal matters by a teacher who was not a Christian. The truth is, we would more readily risk them in the former case, than in the latter. Have not many moral, though unconverted teachers, not only received good themselves, but done good in the Sabbath School? We know that some rotten and rickety ships have crossed the ocean. We know that some stupid, untrained, or drunken captains have succeeded in reaching the desired port. But who would argue from such facts, that such ships and such men should be encouraged to go to sea? They may go to sea, but is it not a tempting of Providence? So, such teachers may enter the Sabbath School, but, all things considered, is it not a tempting of Providence?—Rev. Robert Hood.

THE BIBLE AND THE SUNDAY SCHOOL. 123

(9.) Promises recited by officers and teachers.
(10.) Prayer.
(11.) Notices, Reports and Collections.
(12.) Bible Study.
(13.) Five minutes signal for closing with soft organ voluntary.
(14.) General Review of the lesson by pastor or superintendent, with responsive reading of the lesson.
(15.) Lesson Hymn.
(16.) Dismission by classes, all singing.
(17.) Library books and papers received in the vestibule.
(18.) Enquiry Meeting.

---

5. Financial System for the Sunday School.

BY REV. F. H. MARLING.

An example of what a school may do, which is trained to systematic and intelligent giving, is that of the Fourteenth-street Presbyterian Church of New York City, Mr. Frank A. Ferris, Superintendent. For the last sixteen years it has given an annual average of $1,000. Out of an average attendance for one year of one hundred and forty-seven (exclusive of a large primary class, which also contributed regularly), one hundred and forty-four brought a weekly offering. These donations were entirely for the support of missions.

The record of the amount of missionary money is kept with the same regularity as the record of attendance; indeed, the attendance is marked by the amount of missionary money brought. A large and durable envelope, containing a paper for a list of names, is provided for each class. Opposite the names are spaces for the dates of the Sabbaths in one quarter, and a large space for the scholars' residences. Each Sabbath, when the attendance is taken, the missionary money is collected, and the amount which each child has brought is checked off against his name. If he has been careless and forgotten his money, a cipher marks his presence. All absentees are indicated by the space being left blank. At the foot of the space for each Sunday the amount of missionary money is written, and also the number of absentees. The money is then put into the envelope with the class list, and laid aside to be collected by the secretary at an appropriate time. One excellent feature about Mr. Ferris's system is that there is also a space provided in the class list for the teacher to keep an account of the missionary money he brings. In this, as in all other things, nothing speaks more effectively than example.

The absence of members of the Sunday School during the summer is not allowed to interfere with the regularity of benevolent offerings, a small envelope being furnished especially for this purpose to each person.

A WEEKLY OFFERING

From ....

Class of ....

TO BE USED BY THE

Sabbath School Missionary Association of the 14th Street Presbyterian Church.

Date....	June.	July.				August.				September.	
	28	5	12	19	26	2	9	16	23	30	6	13
Amount..												

TOTAL............

6. Sunday School Music.*

BY P. P. BLISS.†

That which ought to have the greatest emphasis just now in regard to sacred music is **the need of greater reverence**. While a song is being sung people will pass up a Church aisle or a Sunday School aisle, whisper to each other, move about a room, distribute or collect library books, put on overcoats (if it is a closing song), do a score of **things that one would never think of doing during any other kind of prayer**. When we are offering praise or prayer to God, whether in metre or without it, a reverence of manner and of spirit should accompany it. Another thing to be enforced, kindred to that we have mentioned, is a greater thoughtfulness of the real meaning of the words we sing. Are they the words of prayer? Of praise? Let an appropriate thought, as well as melody, accompany them. Let songs sometimes be explained or developed, as a Sunday School lesson would be, to show the fulness of thought and meaning.

Singing in the Primary Class.‡

BY MRS. W. F. CRAFTS.

(1.) **Sing Worshipfully.** Make the children understand that they are to sing to God, not to their teacher or to each other. Keep the idea of praise continually before their minds

---

* "Trophies of Song," published by D. Lothrop & Co., Boston (price $1 25), gives many valuable hints in regard to the use of Sacred Music in Church and Sunday School, with 200 incidents about popular hymns that may be used with great profit to show the origin and power of various songs.

† Author of "Gospel Songs"—one of the very best collections of songs for Sunday Schools, Prayer Meetings, &c. Published by John Church, Cincinnati, Ohio.

‡ Songs for Little Folks, by Mrs. W. F. Crafts and Miss Jennie Merrill, about two hundred songs for use in the Sunday School, day school, home and Kindergarten. Biglow & Main, Publishers. For sale by the publisher of this book. Price in boards, $30 per 100 copies. Single copy 35 cents, one copy in paper cover by mail, 25 cents.

by such reminders as the following :—"God likes you to think about what you are singing to Him." "God's little birds make more music than you do. Certainly you can sing as well for Him as they do."

(2.) **Explain the hymn** before it is sung, so that the children may sing with the heart and with the understanding. Make them feel what they sing. Teach them to be as reverential in song as in prayer.

(3.) **The Song should be simple but not silly.** It should contain not pretty jingle but gospel truth. Many of the grand old hymns of the church can be brought within the child's comprehension by means of illustration and explanation.

(4.) **The compass of the song** should not be high, "never above E flat." It should be cheerful in the words and in the melody.

(5.) **Action Songs** are very appropriate for the Primary Class. When the children are permitted to express in motions what they are singing, they will understand and feel more deeply what they sing, for instance, if they sing about the rain, let them imitate the rain by pattering on a hard surface with their finger tips. If they sing about the snow, let their little hands represent the snowflakes. The action songs are also very helpful because they give the necessary change of positions, and thus promote good order.

---

7. SUNDAY SCHOOL CONCERTS.

BY REV. W. F. CRAFTS.

A Sunday School Concert should have three qualities :—

(1.) **Unity.** Songs, Scripture and recitation should all be on *one theme*, *e. g.*, "The Cross," "The Promises," "The Snow,"* "Trees of the Bible," "Mountains of the Bible," &c.

---

* An illustrated Concert on "The Treasures of the Snow" published by D. Lothrop & Co., Boston, was explained, with pictures of snowflakes magnified and enlarged,

(2.) **Instructiveness.** A Concert may be full of instruction without being any less popular and spiritual for that reason. The historical associations of Bible "trees and mountains" would nobly prepare the way for spiritual work.

(3.) **Spirituality.** A Concert, just as surely as a Sermon, or lesson of the Sunday School, should be pervaded and crowned with spiritual impressions; *e. g.*, after showing God's wisdom as seen in the snow, and also His power, His grace may be emphasized, as typified by the snow, and a powerful spiritual impression be left on the audience, many of whom would not come to hear a formal "Sermon."

---

8. Specimen of Printing Press Helps for the Sunday School.

(1) INVITATIONS TO ATTENDANCE.

"Search the Scriptures."

Broadway Congregational Sunday School,

NORWICH, CONN.

FOR THE YOUNG AND THE OLD.

Session each Sabbath at 3.00 P.M.

A corps of earnest Christian Teachers will heartily welcome to their Classes all who desire to study the Bible.

Adult Members of our Church and Congregation are earnestly invited to become Members of the Bible Classes of our School. Will YOU encourage us by your presence next Sabbath?

W. R. BURNHAM,
Superintendent.

"Thy Word is Truth." "Thy Word is Pure."

"Thy Word is a Lamp unto my Feet."

"The entrance of Thy Word giveth light."—Ps. 9.

Western Avenue Baptist Sunday School.

The Bible-Studying Department of the Church.

H. R. CLISSOLD, SUPERINTENDENT.

Services begin at Half-past Two o'clock.

COME.

BETHANY

Offers a friendly hand to the Man or Woman, Boy or Girl, who is not attending any place of worship REGULARLY, and in the New Building the Pastor and Superintendent will try to make each one feel at home among friends. The Rooms for Adult Bible Classes have in each of them good teachers, and any person can join without any ceremony. Enter any room, take any seat, and find a welcome,

2.30 EVERY SABBATH AFTERNOON.

	High Street.	West Street.		Broom Street.	Prince Street.
Kinney St......					
Baldwin St......			CHAPEL[ ]		
Marshall St.....					
Scriber's Lane			Grand St.		
Court St.........					

(2) Reception and Record of New Members.

Wesley Chapel M. E. Bible School,

Davenport Avenue, corner Ward Street.

New Haven, ... *187*

....*has to-day* applied *for admission to Membership in our School, and if it is also* **YOUR** *wish that*..................*join us, please do me the favor to* **FILL UP AND SIGN** *the blank below, that we may from it make our School Record.*

Be assured, dear friend, if you see fit to commit your .... to our care, we shall seek, by the help of the Master, to do .... what good we can, and will gladly welcome you also as **Members** or **Visitors** at our School Sessions.

Yours very truly,

JNO. E. SEARLES, Jr.,
Superintendent.

Full Name of Scholar, ...
Age, ...Residence, ...
Church attended by Parents, ...
Your signature, ...

(3) Letters to Teachers and Scholars.

"Whatsoever He saith unto you, do it."

"Search the Scriptures; for in them ye think ye have eternal life: and they are they which testify of me."

Sabbath School, Congregational Church,

Washington, D.C. 187

Dear Fellow-Laborer,

The regular Teachers' Meeting for the study of the Lesson for the next Lord's Day, will be held at _____ St.

Will you not come, and sit with us at the feet of the blessed Master? Bring any of your friends.

Affectionately Yours,

O. F. PRESBREY,
S. S. Superintendent.

"Whatsoever ye do, do it heartily as to the Lord and not unto man."

'Go ye also into the vineyard, and whatsoever is right, I will give you."

Teachers' Sociable.

Compliments of W. J. Duncan to the Teachers

OF THE

Chestnut Street Baptist Sabbath School,

FOR

....Evening,..................................187

AT

METHODIST EPISCOPAL SUNDAY SCHOOL.

SEDALIA, Mo., ... 187

    Dear friend and scholar,—Grace, mercy, and peace. from God the Father, and our Lord Jesus Christ.

    I was sorry when I had to mark you absent from your class last Sabbath. Are you sick ?

    Our lesson for next Sunday is ....

    The topic, ...

    The golden text, ...

    Come, regardless of the weather, if your health will permit, and study with us God's blessed Word, which is full of precious promises to you.

                Your friend and teacher,

                  Remember the hour—9.30 *a.m.*

(4) Secretary's Blank.

Philadelphia, ... *187*

Superintendent.

Weather, ...

OPENING EXERCISES.

ATTENDANCE.

		Main Floor.	Class Room.	Primary Room.	Infant Room.	Officers.	Total.
SCHOLARS	Male....						
	Female.						
TEACHERS	Male........						
	Female.....						

Visitors........
Grand Total....

CLOSING EXERCISES.

BLACK BOARD LESSON.

REMARKS.

9. Organization of the Primary Class.

BY MRS. W. F. CRAFTS.

Does your class number a hundred scholars, more or less, and are you perplexed to know how to keep the attendance of so many; how to tell whom you ought to visit on account of absence or sickness; how to learn not only their names, but also their souls' needs; how to give each child a personal share in the lesson time; how to get the interest and attention of all; how to save the distraction and trouble required to hush a noise here and quiet a child there; how to judge of the effect of your lesson upon each little heart; how to make each child feel that you are his special friend for Christ's sake. These questions are all answered in the following plan.

Separate the little people into knots of ten, endeavoring to put those of like capacity together. While age may be some guide in this matter of grading, the most important consideration is a child's power to understand. It may be necessary to form more than one class of the same grade. It would be better to have less than ten in a class than more.

Give each little group a teacher who will have them in charge during twenty minutes of the session, in which time the attendance is marked, the collection taken, and specified portions of the lesson taught. Thus each child will receive in the class close and personal attention, which should also be extended to the home by visiting during the week, especially in case of absence or sickness.

One of the greatest advantages of this class system is found in connection with **transfers to the general school.** Instead of having those who are transferred scattered promiscuously through various classes with strange teachers and strange classmates, or even placed together under the same teacher, but a new one, the mature classes may be transferred at appropriate times with their teachers, thus keeping the relations of growing interest and affection unbroken. As a rule, transfer children at about eight years of age.

10. The Value and Use of Sociables.

AN INSTITUTE CONVERSATION.

(1) **Convention Sociables.** During Conventions and institutes it is found beneficial, during long sessions, to have one or more brief recesses for conversation and becoming better acquainted.

(2) **Superintendents' Sociables** are of great value. The Superintendents of a city, or county, or district, meet in a church parlor, or private parlor, and spend a portion of an evening sociably in conversation, a portion around the refreshment table, and a further portion in discussing some topic of special interest to Superintendents.

(3) **Primary Class Parties** at the teacher's home afford great delight and profit. At one time let it be a "bird party," with Bible birds, stuffed and in pictures; at another time let it be a "grape party," a "cherry party," &c., gratifying the child's love of variety.

(4) **Young Ladies' Sewing Circles** at the teacher's home may be made delightful for young ladies' classes or young girls.

(5) **Five Minute Sociables** before the opening of the Sunday School for each class would be both pleasant and profitable, enabling the teacher to teach with better sympathy and adaptation.

---

11. An Ancient Religious Convention.

NOW these are they that came to David . . . and they were among the mighty men, **helpers of the war.**

These were . . . captains of the host: one of the least was over a hundred, and the greatest over a thousand. . .

And David went out to meet them, and answered and said unto them, If ye be come peaceably unto me to help me, mine heart shall be knit unto you. . . . , then **the spirit** came upon Amasai, who was chief of the captains, and he said, Thine are we, David, and on thy side, thou son of Jesse: peace, peace be unto thee, and peace be to thine helpers; for **thy God helpeth thee.** Then David received them, and made them captains of the band. And they helped David . . . . : for they were all mighty men of valor, and were captains in the host.

For at that time day by day there came to David to help him, until it was a great host, like the host of God.

And these . . . ready armed to the war came to David, . . mighty men of valor, famous throughout the house of their father; . . . **men that had understanding of the times, to know what Israel ought to do**; the heads of them were two hundred, . . . **expert in war, with all instruments of war: . . . they were not of double heart.**

And there they were with David three days, eating and drinking: for their brethren had prepared for them. Moreover they that were nigh them, . . . brought bread . . . and meat, meal, cakes of figs, and bunches of raisins, . . . and oil, and oxen, and sheep, abundantly: for there was joy in Israel.

And David consulted with the captains of thousands and hundreds, and with every leader. And David said unto all the congregation of Israel, If it seem good unto you, and that it be of the Lord our God, let us send abroad unto our brethren everywhere, that are left in all the land of Israel, and with them also to the priests and Levites which are in their cities and suburbs, that they may gather themselves unto us: And let us **bring again the ark of our God to us**. . . .

And all the congregation said that they would do so: for the thing was right in the eyes of all the people.

So David gathered all Israel together, ... to bring the ark of God from Kirjathjearim. . . . .

And David and all Israel played before God with all their might, and **with singing**, and with harps, and with psalteries, and with timbrels, and with cymbals, and with trumpets.—1 Chron. xii, xiii.

VI. THE BIBLE AND THE WORLD.

1. THE BIBLE AND THE PUBLIC SCHOOLS.

BY REV. C. H. PAYNE, D.D.

WHAT THE QUESTION IS NOT.

(1.) It is not a question of the union of Church and State, much less of sectarian domination over State institutions.

(2.) It is not a question of *enforcing* even religious instruction, much less sectarian teaching, compulsorily upon all pupils in the public schools of our country.

(3.) It is not a question of the simple reading of a few verses from the Bible in a formal manner, at the opening of our public schools, set over against the peril or probable destruction of the public school system.

THE REAL ISSUE.

The question comes to us in this practical form: Shall the Bible be kept in the public schools permissively as undeniably the best text book of moral instruction extant, or shall it be expelled by *prohibitory* legislation, or proscriptive action of school officials?

In discussing this issue, another question ought to be our guide, namely, **Which course, the retention or the expulsion of the Bible, is likely to be attended with the greatest good and the least peril to the schools themselves and the nation?** "The greatest good to the greatest number" is a fair and honorable principle to apply to this pregnant question.

REASONS FOR RETAINING THE BIBLE.

(1.) The Bible, thus retained as a moral text book, can work no real harm to any individual, or to the State; while its expulsion, to say the least, is hazardous to both. It can not be justly claimed that the Bible in the schools inflicts actual injury to any one. The most that is claimed is that it conflicts with the *views* of certain parties. If this were a serious evil, it might be obviated by adjusting the Bible-reading so as not to make this exercise compulsory as regards every pupil. To expel the Bible for so slight a cause seems the highest unwisdom.

THE CHRISTIAN CHARACTER OF THE NATION.

(2.) The expulsion of the Bible by prohibitory enactment would be a *new departure*, in opposition to our entire national history, policy and spirit.

Nothing is clearer than that the theory and practice of our Government hitherto have not been that of entire secularism; nothing more evident than that we are, in the truest sense of the word, a Christian nation. That this palpable fact should be denied or questioned by any one acquainted with our national history is almost inexplicable. It argues nothing against this fact that the nation and the Church are not inseparably joined in *legal bonds*, nor that the fact is not stated in formal terms in the Constitution. Without this, it remains a potent and undeniable fact, that fundamentally, traditionally, historically, practically, we are a Christian nation.

Abundant evidence might be adduced: not to emphasize the Pilgrim founders of the nation, with their revered Bible and their holy Sabbath, and their constant mingling of the sacred with the secular, possibly with too much rigidness, there remain the opening of the Continental Congress with prayer, the resolutions authorizing the importing of twenty thousand copies of the Bible, approving and encouraging the publication of an edition of the Scriptures, resolutions against profanity, appointing days of fasting, prayer and thanksgiving, in which God, Christ, and the Christian religion are distinctly and repeatedly recognised. Our present Congress and State Legislatures publicly recognise Christianity, by religious worship and the observance of the Christian Sabbath. During the civil war, in 1863, the national Senate passed a resolution, "devoutly recognising the supreme authority and just government of Almighty God in all the affairs of men and of nations," and calling upon the people, " in this day of trouble, by the assurance of His Word, to seek Him for succor, according to His appointed way, through Jesus Christ." Have we one faith or religion for times of trouble, and another or none for times of peace ? The Christian religion is recognised in our courts of justice, in the army and navy, and on the statutes of our Legislatures. In several States it has been declared to be the common law. A decision of the court in New York says of Christianity : " It is, in fact, the religion of the people and ever has been, and has been so recognised from the first by Constitutional Conventions, Legislatures, and courts of justice." A recent decision of the same State is of the same character. Judge Story, speaking of the Constitution, and the reason why Christianity has no more formal and legal place in it, says : " An attempt to level all religions, and make it a matter of State policy to hold all in utter indifference, would have created universal disapprobation." Yet, in the face of facts like these, which might be multiplied *ad libitum*, it is proposed that our nation suddenly change its policy—a policy which has made it what it is, given it its prestige, prosperity, and power—and assume an attitude of avowed indifference to Christianity, and *virtual opposition* to the Bible. A change so radical in character, so far-reaching in results, if affecting merely civil and political interests, would never be made by wise statesmen, except the gravest and most certain peril demanded it. How much more should we pause and ponder when the proposed change reaches to the very foundations of the Government, affects the most vital interests of the national well-being, morality, and religion !

It is a serious matter for a nation to depart from the teachings of so wise and revered a man as Washington ; it is inexpressibly serious for it to set at naught the wisdom of God's Word, and array itself in hostility to that Being whose protection it has hitherto sought, and by whose favor it has risen to its lofty prominence among the nations of earth. Let it not be replied that the nation proposes no such sweeping departure. I reply, it is all involved in the proposition now so prominently before the country.

ANTAGONISM OF CHRISTIANITY AND THE STATE THE SEQUENCE OF THIS MOVEMENT.

3. And this leads me to the statement of another and more potent reason why I am opposed to expelling the Bible from our Public Schools, namely, because the reasons alleged, and the arguments adduced therefor, if followed to their legitimate sequences, will inevitably place this nation in direct antagonism to the Christian religion, and foster a spirit of atheism and infidelity fatally destructive to its highest interests. Understand me. I do not charge that this is the thought or purpose of any considerable number who advocate this policy. I simply affirm that it is the logical result, and will be the practical working of the system when carried out as proposed.

As I have before stated, it is not the simple matter of the formal reading of a few passages from the Bible, though even that may have a far more potent influence on the youth of our land than is apparent at first thought. But **the question, when reduced to its last analysis, which form it is rapidly assuming, is this : Shall Christianity be abolished from our national life?** Of course, by national life I do not mean the life of every man in the nation, but the nation as such in its national capacity. Shall it continue, as in the past, to recognise Christianity as, in a general sense, the religion of the people, and, as heretofore, conform the national administration to the general spirit and requirements of Christianity ? or shall it cease all such recognition and conformity, and become equally indifferent to all religions and no religion ? This, I repeat, is the real issue, which we must not suffer ourselves to lose sight of in the wordy strife about minor issues, nor accept any mere denial of it. Let us, rather, carefully and impartially examine for ourselves **the positions and arguments of the advocates of expulsion**, and see whither they must lead the nation, and what must be their logical results.

It is asserted that the State should assume the position of absolute *separatism from all religion*, and stand upon the platform of utter *secularism*, equally favorable or neutral to every form of religious faith or unfaith, and treating all with unqualified impartiality. " Hands off " are the two expressive words which "summarize " the new policy that the State is urged to adopt toward all religions. And this theory has in it a semblance of equity and wisdom at first view. But let us see what it will lead to when applied to our nation in its present relations to Christianity. The State honestly accepting this doctrine must at once assume the aggressive in a *direct attack* upon Christian institutions, laws, and usages. It must begin this fearful work of demolition on its own structure; tear up its own strong foundations, which were laid in sacrifices, toils, and tears, and cemented with blood; pull down its own grand pillars of strength and beauty, which have so long supported the national edifice; go through the sacred national temple, so long revered, scourge in hand, to drive out, not those who defile it by godlessness, extortion, corruption, and the whole vile brood of unchristian parasites, but to expel every fair and beautiful form that bears the legend " Christian " on its chaste brow; every law transcribed from the higher code sent down to us from heaven; every custom derived from God's Book, and garlanded with flowers of celestial beauty. Ah, what a mission is this on which to send the pure goddess of our loved Republic? Say not this is an unwarranted figure of speech, overstating the issue. Not so. Carry out the theory proposed, and the nation must cease to recognise Christianity any more than it does Mohammedanism or Buddhism. It must assume the role of *propagandist* of its new policy *against* Christianity. It must be equally just or indifferent toward all religions, repeal every law distinctively Christian from the statutes of the several States; abolish all Sabbath laws, and all national and legislative observance of the Sabbath; take the Bible from every court of justice and State institution; drive every chaplain from the national Congress, legislative halls, the army and navy; and cease all prayer to a God in whom some of its subjects do not believe, and from whom the nation has proposed to itself absolute separation. The President and several Governors of the States must write no more proclamations recognising God; appoint no more fast days or thanksgivings; and if, as not many years agone, national calamity should again befall us, and the black cloud of war cast its awful shadow over our fair land, and our noble sons fall by thousands into bloody graves, there must be no more invoking the "God of our fathers;" for times have changed, and we have made "progress" and torn off the shackles of "tyrannous customs," and Jehovah is no longer the nation's God; but a *universal nothingness* has been set on His throne, and the people must make their moan and shed their tears and bury their slaughtered dead, with no national appeal to the "God of Battles" to stay the scourge and save the imperilled nation.

This doctrine of State neutrality and utter separation from the Church is delusive. In our wholesome zeal against the formal legal union of Church and State, we are in danger of swinging over to a rash and untenable extreme.

It is claimed that the Bible itself teaches this doctrine—that Christianity, being a spiritual religion, must win its way entirely by spiritual forces. A half truth misapplied to the question at issue. If it means anything in this connection, it means that the State is to have *nothing to do* with religion, and religion is to have *nothing to do* with the State.

The Church has an imperative command to propagate the Gospel. How, if not by aid of civil authority? Her missionaries stand before the turreted walls of China or Japan with their closed and guarded gates. How shall they gain ingress with God's Book and message of salvation, except through treaty stipulation by the government of which they are subjects? But this is virtually in violation of the doctrine of non-interference and neutrality on the part of the State, and non-reliance on government aid on the part of the Church.

As a matter of fact the State does, and must, maintain a somewhat intimate connection with the Church. No Church organization is formed but the State regulates the appointment of its trustees and the tenure of its property. There is a wide difference between *enforcing* religion and *recognising* it. The one it may not do; the other it may and must. But the argument, by which it is sought to strengthen the demand for expelling the Bible, claims that the State shall not *recognise* the Christian religion because, forsooth, it can not equally recognise any and every religion which a few of its subjects may choose to adopt. The principle being a false one, either wholly impracticable or wholly destructive of Christianity in the national life, the argument becomes invalid, and the Bible should remain in its stronghold unaffected by the false and faulty reasoning.

WHAT THE CONSCIENCE ARGUMENT AMOUNTS TO.

Equally false in principle and impracticable in application is **the argument for expelling the Bible from our schools because its reading is said to be offensive to the consciences of some parties.** Here, again, we have a seeming truth overlying a fatal error. The theory that the Government must accommodate its laws and administration to the consciences of its several subjects is untenable and subversive of the very ends of government. What kind of a government would that be that was adjusted to the universal conscience of its subjects? What laws could it make and enforce? A law against polygamy would be very offensive to the consciences of the Utah saints. Shall this disgraceful blot upon our civilization thus be encouraged by the nation, and no legal barrier raised against its spread, out of respect to the consciences of its adherents? Such must be the attitude of the Government, if the conscience argument is valid. So, many consciences are offended by a law inflicting capital punishment for murder. Must the nation prohibit the enactment of such laws, or the State respect the consciences of such so as to repeal existing laws for their accommodation? The conscience of the Communist is offended by the rich man's hoarded capital, while the poor man lacks for bread, and so he demands laws of equalization. Nay, there are multiplied thousands of poor men in this country who are grievously offended at the supposed inequality which exists between capital and labor—the rich and the poor—and the clamor for what is called justice and equality is becoming more and more serious. Shall the Government undertake to accommodate itself to every man's conscience in regard to this vital subject, pass agrarian laws, and establish a community of goods? Will that portion of the press, which is so zealous in advocating this universal conscience argument, carry it forward in its application to these and similar questions? The Chinese conscience is opposed to telegraph lines. They have a religious superstition respecting them, and believe them the source of incalculable spiritual evil, so that a telegraph wire will not be tolerated in China. Ought not our Government to respect the consciences of these honest, hard-working subjects, and forbid the erection of telegraph lines? nay, demolish those already established? Do you smile and say, if the Chinese don't like our telegraphs let them return to China, whence they came, and not expect us to conform our laws and usages to their beliefs? Ah, well, that would seem to be a very fair way of putting the case; but let that same argument be applied to those who oppose the Bible in the schools and the observance of the Sabbath, and other usages of our Christian civilization, and the cry of bigotry, sectarianism, and persecution is raised. That, certainly, is a poor principle which can not be equally applied to questions of similar character. There is yet another and quite numerous class of our people—not the latest comers of our free land, but among the earliest and worthiest of the nation's subjects—whose consciences are offended by the practice of war. Is it the policy of the Government not to conflict with the conscientious and religious belief of these, its excellent Quaker subjects? Where would our nation have been to-day had such been its policy? A broken, ruined, buried republic. Does any one reply, "The State does not force them to bear arms?" Neither does it enforce, or propose to enforce, the actual reading of the Bible upon any one conscientiously opposed to it. The parity of reasoning is this: The State does not abandon its war policy—abolish its army and navy—because of the Quaker's conscience, and it *taxes him* for the expenses of a war waged for the national good. Precisely this has been its policy in regard to the Bible in the public schools, and the taxation of all its subjects, irrespective of religious beliefs, for the common good. The fact is, that this **entire conscience argument fails and falls the mo-**

ment it is subjected to logical and practical tests. The State, in order to its own safety and perpetuity, must rise, not merely above the prejudices and superstitions of many of its subjects, but above their varying individual consciences as well. In other words, there must be a national policy, based upon a national conscience, to secure national prosperity. Yet this weak and utterly indefensible argument is the chief and strongest one employed in the campaign against the Bible in our schools. Can you or I accept as valid a reason which we see to be so absolutely shallow and groundless?

THE LEGAL POSITION EXAMINED.

Let us look at the reason alleged for expelling the Bible from the public school on the principle that it is unjust to tax the Catholics, and others, for the support of a system in which there is anything conflicting with their consciences. This is the ground taken by distinguished authority, when the question was directly before you in the courts in this State. It was affirmed that the Catholics were "punished, every year, for believing as they do, to the extent of two hundred thousand dollars, and to that extent those of us who send our children to these excellent common schools become beneficiaries of the Catholic money." This is held up in the light of injustice, if not absolute dishonesty. The principle, then, is clearly announced that the State ought not to impose a tax upon any of its subjects for the maintenance of that which offends their consciences.

I have already shown how this principle applies to the Quakers and their anti-war belief, and how the Government does not, and can not, change its policy for them. I will now go one step further, and show how the application of this principle will inevitably destroy our entire common school system itself; for these very Catholics, to whom this concession has been made in Cincinatti, chiefly for the very reason alleged above, are **just as conscientiously opposed to the common schools themselves, without the Bible.** Nay, that is the chief object of Catholic opposition—the so-called godless education of their children in secular common schools. To quote Catholic authorities on this point were almost to insult

J

your intelligence. The Pope declares such education outside of the Church to be a "damnable heresy." Archbishop Purcell affirms: "We, as Catholics, can not approve that system of education for youth which is apart from instruction in the Catholic faith and the teaching of the Church," and charges his clergy to admit no boy or girl to "first communion who will not have attended a Catholic school for two years before," etc. This is the position taken by their chief clergy, and leading official Church organs. A true Catholic would prefer our version of the Scriptures in the school to an absolutely secular and godless education. Now the argument used so effectively in favor of removing the Bible, because is was unjust to impose a tax upon the Catholics against their conscience, applies with equal, and even greater force to the public school itself; and when applied, as it is now clamorously demanded, and will be pressed with the indomitable zeal which characterizes that Church, the irresistible logic of the application is this—either we must remove the school tax from the Catholics, and all other persons who feel their consciences oppressed, or divide the school fund with them and all other denominations demanding it. In either case the common school system goes down in completest and most hopeless ruin. For Jew, German, Infidel, Presbyterian, Methodist, and Quaker have an equal right to relief from taxation or division of money with the Catholic.

Strange that acute minds in using this argument of unjust taxation could not see that they used a two-edged sword which in the hands of those for whose defence it was drawn would smite the cherished common school to the very death. Thus is it ever with unguarded concessions to unreasonable though popular demands. The concessions quell the clamor for a moment, only to give it new strength, and new weapons of warfare more destructive and fatal. What was gained by the concession made in Cincinatti by expelling the Holy Book of God from the schools? Were the Catholics better pleased or satisfied? A teacher in one of the city schools informed me that in one month, a year and a half ago, over two hundred Catholic children were removed from his school. The priest had been through his district, and demanded that Catholic parents should withdraw their children from the Public Schools, though there was no offensive Bible-reading in the schools at that time. True, many of these have since returned, because priestly vigilance can hardly prevent all Catholic youth from improving the superior advantages offered in our excellent school system. Again, I ask, shall we accept arguments for the expulsion of the Bible, which carry with them such fatal logical results?

THE RESULT OF ANTI-BIBLE LAWS ON THE SCHOOLS.

Prohibit the Bible in the Common Schools because of its religious teachings, and you adopt a principle which, carried to its logical and practical results, will **entirely revolutionize our present text-books and methods of teaching, produce endless discord in our Public Schools**, and render their continuance an impossibility. It is not the bound volume called the Bible to which objection is made. It is the teachings of the Bible in whatever form presented. A manual of devotional and moral excerpts from the inspired volume would be as objectionable. Any book that in any way inculcates the Christian religion must and will come under the ban of this proscribing principle. And if there be truth or force in the principle, it ought to be rigorously and universally applied. Every reader, every text-book of history, physiology, astronomy, or any other study, that has in it any extracts from God's Word, any Christian teaching, any allusion to God, indeed, as the Supreme Being, is an offensive form of religious teaching, and must be prohibited, or some one's conscience is offended. What a wholesale process of expurgation in our text-books is thus demanded by the inevitable logic of our new and much-vaunted principles of no religious teaching in the Public Schools! How easy it is to use words without considering their meaning; to advocate and inaugurate measures without reflecting upon their results! The very imprint in the text-books of our schools is itself a most decided and emphatic teaching of a "religious tenet"—A.D.; what is it but the most potent and triumphant argument for the Christian religion, flaunted most offensively in the face of every pupil, be he from atheist, Jew, or pagan household?

The practical result of this style of argument is already being realized, and is full of evil portent.

A certain school board passed a resolution that "no religious, pagan or atheistic tenets" should be taught in the schools under their control. A Chinese boy was overheard by the teacher using the most horrible oaths. The teacher kindly reprimanded him, and two days afterwards received a note from one of the School Board, *reprimanding her* for her laudable efforts to correct the boy's fearful profanity, the note closing thus : "You must see that this is entirely inconsistent with the recent resolution of the Board, prohibiting you from teaching religious, pagan, or atheistic tenets. If your course is persisted in, I shall be compelled to bring the matter to the attention of the Board." The teacher sends the statement of facts and the letter to the editor of a religious paper, and asks what she shall do. Yes, that *is* the question which will soon be asked by thousands of teachers all over the country, and by thousands of parents, too, who do not care to have their children educated in a school where profanity must not be mildly corrected, and the name of God cannot be *reverently* uttered.

BIBLE-LOVING PEOPLE ALSO HAVE CONSCIENCES.

There are other people than Catholics and Atheists who have consciences, and who would prefer to have their children educated with *well instructed* consciences; and if the Public School is to become such a hot-bed of infidelity and vice as is here but dimly foreshadowed, these will also let their voice be heard, and, if in vain, the Public School will be abandoned to totter into quick decay, as it ought when robbed of its fairest and worthiest features.

Teachers in Cincinatti have been subjected to most unjust persecution for illustrating the evidence of benevolent design in the human system, in classes studying physiology. The Supreme God is already proscribed from some of the schools, and the fearful process of atheizing our youth will go on, unless we resist it with a unanimity and energy not yet manifested.

THE TRUE POLICY.

4. What, then, is the one only course of wisdom and of safety? This, surely: Let the Bible be an unprescribed text-

book in our Public Schools, with its priceless teachings and its silent yet potent influence; and if any are conscientiously opposed to reading it let them be excused. But, for the sake of the nation and the schools and youth of our country, lay no rude hand of prohibition on God's Holy Word. **No expulsion, no compulsion, is the true policy.** The plea that the Bible is a sectarian book is utterly unfounded. How any Protestant can accept such a charge is inexplicable. The admission is fatal to its claims of Divine authority and universal acceptance. Such admission puts it on a level with the Koran, and other so-called sacred books. It is a message from the universal God to universal man. The fact that all men have not yet accepted it as such, changes not its character, abates nothing from its claims or authority. On no other theory can it be urged on all men every where. I am amazed that a believer in the divinely-inspired volume should admit it to be a sectarian book. The difference between the Douay version and that in common use is but slight, not fundamental. No, it is Jehovah's own Book, who is no sectarist, but the all-Creator, all-Father, the eternal and sovereign God of the universe.

Let the nation also maintain its past and present Christian status, to abandon which would be at infinite peril. No injustice is thus done to any man, because all its subjects came under our national ægis when it bore the Christian sign. The partnership argument, to the effect that every latest comer is a member of the national firm, on equal footing with all the others, and because voluntarily seeking the protection of our Government, and paying a meagre tax for priceless privileges enjoyed, he is therefore entitled to full power and liberty to change our entire national structure, will hardly stand the test of close scrutiny. It should not be forgotten that some things were established before the new partners were admitted, and they came with full knowledge of our national character and institutions. Yes, let them come, one and all, from every land into the partnership of liberty's grand heritage, if they will— but **come to enjoy and not destroy**, the costly boon. Shall not these be the changeless conditions on which all shall come and all remain : the Bible in the Public Schools intact—the nation's text-book, and the nation's chart and charter, with the national historic Christian faith inviolate and perpetual ?

---

2. The Bible and Temperance.*

Miss Frances E. Willard, of Chicago, gave one of those eloquent, thoughtful and impassioned addresses which she so well knows how to deliver. She told how her heart had been aroused when the women went crusading two years ago ; how she threw aside her books and found the salvation of human souls more precious than literature and art. She claimed of voters protection for our homes, our women and children, and the institutions of our native land from the rum-demon ; of the odds against us in a cause where there are twelve grog-shops for one church, twelve barkeepers for one minister. She spoke of the happiness of engaging in the work, and of the beauty of the term "lady," not only as a giver of bread, its old Saxon meaning, but also as the giver of the bread of life. She said : "If it is good to work as a sculptor in the plastic clay and chiseled marble, it is better to mould the hearts of humanity ; if it is well to paint with the brush of the artist, it is better to restore the image of God in faces which have lost it. If it is good to study the architecture of the mediæval world, it is better to teach about the great Temple of which men are the living stones ; if it is sweet to study the laws of musical tones, it is better to evoke the music of the heart's Æolian harp. And I am happier to remember day by day that Jack, the sailor on Lake Michigan, is praying for me than if I stood in the foremost rank of what all the world call rich and noble." Miss Willard then told of the last charge of her only sister—whose life and death she has embodied in her little volume entitled "Nineteen Beautiful Years ;" which she delivered to her audience. "*I want you to tell every one to be good.*"

---

* We are unable to give the addresses on Temperance in the direct form in which we have put the other points. Charles M. Morton, pastor of Plymouth Bethel, spoke powerfully on "The Need of Christian Temperance Work," from the standpoint of his own experience. Rev. S. L. Gracey eloquently described the Christian Reform Club movement of New England.

THE BIBLE AND THE SUNDAY SCHOOL. 151

3. THE BIBLE AND UNIVERSAL BROTHERHOOD.*

We desire to mention in this connection the Foreign Sunday School Association of which Mr. Albert Woodruff, of New York, is President, whose work is to establish Sunday Schools on the continent of Europe, where until recently they were unknown, being introduced by Mr. Woodruff himself. The work is one of the noblest and wisest of missionary agencies, and ought to receive from the Sunday Schools of Canada and the United States, a generous financial support. As we reach the children of Europe, we shape its future, and in no way can the rationalism and superstition of those old Kingdoms be more surely counteracted than by the planting of these Christian "Childrens' Services" as they are called. —W. F. C.

ARISE AND SHINE.

MARY A. LATHBURY.   P. P. BLISS.

1. Lift up, lift up thy voice with sing-ing, Dear land, with strength lift up . . thy voice! The king-doms of the
2. Yet who, re-nowned in state or sto-ry, Shall en-ter while the King . . host waits? What star at-tract thee

* Psa. cxxxiii.

3. Through wave and wilderness He sought thee,
   For thou wast precious in His sight;
   Shone on thy night of blood, and brought thee
   Through pain and peril to the light.
         Arise and shine, &c.

4. And shall His flock with strife be riven?
   Shall envious lines His church divide,
   When He, the Lord of earth and heaven,
   Stands at the door to claim His bride?
         Arise and shine, &c.

5. Lift up the gates! bring forth oblations
   One crowned with crowns a message brings.
   His word a sword to smite the nations;
   His name—the Christ, the King of kings.
         Arise and shine, &c.

6. He comes! Let all the earth adore Him;
   The path His human nature trod
   Spreads to a royal realm before Him,
   The LIFE of life, the WORD of GOD!
         Arise and shine, &c.

Copyrighted, 1876, by JOHN CHURCH & CO.
Also published in Sheet Music form by

JOHN CHURCH & CO.
Publishers of Sabbath School and Church Music Books,
CINCINNATI, OHIO.

APPENDIX.

SUNDAY SCHOOL PARLIAMENT.

HELD AT THOUSAND ISLAND PARK,

July 18*th*–26*th*, 1876.

BY REV. JESSE LYMAN HURLBUT.

There will soon be need, if there is not already, of a new edition of Webster's Dictionary, to define the new terms of Sunday-school science, and inform the inquiring mind the precise difference between a "Convention," an "Institute," an "Assembly," a "Congress," and a "Parliament." As your correspondent had been present at all these varieties of Sunday-school meeting except th latter, it seem best to complete the chain by a personal inspection of this also, the latest development, especially as it appears likely to be, for a time at least, and perhaps for a lifetime, his only opportunity to be a genuine M. P.

So, one warm afternoon, we packed our valise, shook off for a season the dust of Plainfield, that favored Sunday-school centre, where Vincent dwells occasionally, and Lowry tunes his lyre, where the most illiterate can repeat the names of the Israelite judges, and where the katydids murmur alliterative outlines and robins pipe out "nauseous acrostics." We stepped on board the "St. John," not at all puffed up with the consciousness that while all the rest of the crowd were going to the College regatta, *we* were going to Parliament. We steamed up the lordly Hudson—yes, *steamed* is the word, for it was a night of perspiration in an inside state-room—then followed a dusty day on the railroad, from Albany through Utica, Rome and other cities of ancient fame, to Cape Vincent, where the eyes gazed out upon Lake Ontario on one side, and the broad bosom of the St. Lawrence River upon the other. A steamer was awaiting us, upon whose upper deck we enjoyed the cool breeze and the varied scenery. It was a voyage of two hours down the river, long to be remembered for the splendor of the setting sun, and the loveliness of a changing landscape. The boat wound its tortuous way among the Thousand Islands, some of them large enough for a city, others " no bigger than a baby's head," as one of the voyagers observed. There were islets carpeted with green and shaded by trees, and rocks which jutted out bare and barren from the blue waters; here and there one occupied by a solitary summer cottage, or a little encampment of tents; but for the most part desolate and uninhabited.

At half past seven, just as the grey of twilight was closing around, we saw the white tents and evening lamps gleaming amid the foliage, and knew that we were nearing Wells', or Wellesley Island, as it is variously termed, the seat of the Thousand Islands Park, where is held the Sunday School Parliament. This is one of the largest of the islands in the group, being several miles in length, and in some places a mile wide. There is a rocky wall around it, forming a bluff from ten to a hundred feet high. On this foundation lies a grassy plateau, gradually rising from the wharf inland, so that from almost every point of the encampment the water can be seen. There are clumps of trees, of natural growth, dotting the green sward picturesquely, and supplying abundant shade, where it is ever refreshingly cool. While New Yorkers were sweltering at one hundred degrees, and Philadelphians were broiling at one hundred and five degrees, we Members of Parliament were sitting in comfort at eighty five degrees.

Here, a Camp Meeting Association, of which Chancellor Haven, of Syracuse University, is president, has purchased a thousand acres, and laid out a summer resort of the religio-real-estate quality, and on the plan of magnificent distances. As yet, the camp is in its infancy, but if it survives the present financial crisis (about which its friends feel no anxiety), it is destined to rival Martha's Vineyard and Ocean Grove, for it has great natural attractions, and is under wise business management.

We disembark, and walk up an avenue toward the centre of the Park. On the left is the trustees' office—on the right a building whose size gives promise of quantity, if not of quality, in provisions. It is the dining-hall and its fare is, on the whole, rather better than at the average camp-meeting. Near by stands Wesley Hall, where Conductor (perhaps we ought to say *Speaker*) Crafts reigns, and his guests are domiciled. The rooms are comfortable—for a watering place—though the mattrasses are not of spring, nor the pillows of down, but both of straw. We walk further up the hill and find the Parliament already in its first session—not under the gothic arches of St. Stephen's, but beneath the ample folds of a huge tent, over which wave peacefully side by side the cross of St. George and the starry banner of the Republic. The audience upon the benches (this parliamentary expression fits admirably) is not large, but select. Mr. Speaker Crafts is in the chair, and beside him the Lord Chancellor, not on the woolsack, but on a camp stool. There were speeches of greeting, not only from both sides of the St. Lawrence, but also from both shores of the Atlantic, and from representatives of Sunday-school cause in its various aspects. Mr. John E. Searles, Jr., of New Haven, from the Executive Committee of the International Convention, gave a short and spicy address. Miss M. E. Winslow, (who is not unknown to the readers of the *Times*) spoke about the Foreign Sunday-school with womanly grace and soulful earnestness. Miss Nellie Brown, of Haverhill, N. H., sang several songs, in a rich voice of remarkable power. Then, at the close, a little blind boy of ten years, Charlie Hays, stood up and sang "I love to work for Jesus," in such sweet, sad tones, as brought moisture to many eyes, and the Parliament was duly opened.

Next morning, Wednesday, July 19, the working sessions began in good earnest. Were we to give such a report as the merit of the exercises deserved, an extra number of the *Times* would be needed, for there was a solid week's programme, of which every portion was carried out, and to which some impromptu additions were made. The plan of working was to give a distinct theme to each day, and thus secure at once method and variety. Thus there was a "Teachers' Day," in which we learned how to study a lesson, and how to teach it; why and how the teacher should study, not alone the text-book, but his class: how to employ the blackboard, and how *not* to use it. Next came a "Day of Hard Questions," of which the best feature was a general talk (some literary folks call it a *conversazione*) on "How to manage unruly boys," in which M. C. Hazard, of *The National Sunday School Teacher*, and Charles M. Morton, of Plymouth Bethel, led off with admirable short speeches, in which the principal suggestion about unruly boys seemed to be an infinite patience with them. Friday was devoted to "Childhood." Dr. Latimer, of the Boston Methodist Episcopal School of Theology, delivered an able and scholarly address on the Conversion of Children, and Dr. Richard Newton, of Philadelphia, preached one of his inimitable children's sermons; and there were other speeches, equally valuable, Drs. Castle and Munro, of Canada, besides a lecture by Mr. Crafts. Nor may we omit to mention the Primary Teachers' meeting, with its suggestive talks by Mrs. Crafts and Miss Jennie B. Merrill, of New York. Saturday was allotted to "Sunday School Machinery," with the use of printing press, etc. Sunday was occupied by a sermon by the Rev. Dr. Newton, a Model Sunday School, and in the evening a Temperance Meeting, in which Miss Frances E. Willard spoke with all her accustomed power. Monday, the 24th, had for its theme, "Spiritual Work." Tuesday and Wednesday following, were spent as "Bible Days," with the closing exercises of the meeting.

We have not mentioned half of the good things, nor of the prominent men who were present. The Rev. Messrs. F. H. Marling, H. M. Parsons, Lyman Abbott, the Rev. Dr. Payne, of Ohio, Wesleyan, and a host besides, were on the bill of fare.

Mr. Crafts, though a young man to organize and conduct such a meeting, showed himself master of the occasion, and equal to every emergency, presiding with ease, and leading the discussions with ability. Mrs. Crafts spoke several times on the theme of "Primary classes, and how to conduct them," with complete understanding of her subject, in a ladylike, refined manner, and to the equal pleasure and profit of all who heard her.

There was an atmosphere of devotion and spirituality throughout the meeting. A service of song and prayer opened every day; there were Bible-readings and religious exercises scattered all through the week; and even the printed programme was embroidered with Scripture references. Mr. and Mrs. P. P. Bliss were both present during nearly all the exercises, and that is sufficient assurance that there was spiritual singing which warmed the heart and lifted up the soul.

Let us not forget that Normal class work, the great feature of all our summer Sunday School assemblies, was not neglected. Your correspondent enjoyed the privilege of presenting the subject, both in theory and in practice; and a number of first-class drills were held on various subjects connected with the Bible, and the methods of teaching it.

The programme was so full as to leave little time remaining for those who undertook to "see it through." Yet it is said there were other attractions at Wells' Island beside those under the big tent. Several times we noticed little groups going off towards the shore in a way that was faintly suggestive of fishing. And no wonder, for the waters looked tempting, and we saw strings of pickerel, which were enough to make anybody wish to drop a line down the depths. Indeed, unless our eyes deceived us, we beheld one breezy afternoon, the blue spectacles of our friend Hazard (and they are all that ever is blue about him), in a fishing-boat, and in close proximity to a trolling line. No torture shall wring out of our tongue the tale of how many pickerel and black bass were caught that day. Suffice it to observe, that if any of our readers shall go to the next summer's session of the Parliament, or the Reichstag, or the Cortes, or the Star Chamber, if either of these titles come into vogue by that time, they may still find some little fishes left to be caught in the St. Lawrence River.—*From the Sunday School Times.*

OFFICERS AND SPEAKERS

OF THE

SUNDAY SCHOOL PARLIAMENT.

Rev. W. F. CRAFTS, Conductor.
Mrs. W. F. CRAFTS, Leader of Primary Department.
P. P. BLISS, Leader of Music.
Mrs. P. P. BLISS and Miss NELLIE BROWN,
Musical Assistants.
Rev. S. L. GRACEY and Rev. B. P. RAYMOND,
Institute Secretaries.
Rev. E. O. HAVEN. D.D., LL.D., President of the Association.
Rev. J. F. DAYAN, Secretary, Watertown, N.Y.

Rev. Richard H. Newton, D.D., Editor of *Sunday School World*, Philadelphia.
Rev. J. E. Latimer, D.D., Dean of School of Theology, Boston University.
James Hughes, Esq., Inspector of Schools, Toronto.
Rev. Lyman Abbott, D.D., Editor of *Christian Weekly*, New York.

THE BIBLE AND THE SUNDAY SCHOOL. 159

M. C. Hazard, Esq., Editor of *National Sunday School Teacher*, Chicago.
Rev. C. H. Payne, D.D., President of Ohio Wesleyan University.
Rev. John Potts, D.D., Toronto.
Rev. H. M. Parsons, D.D., Boston.
Rev. Henry Ward Beecher, Brooklyn.
Rev. John N. Castle, D.D., Toronto.
Rev. F. H. Marling, New York.
Charles M. Morton, Plymouth Bethel, Brooklyn.
Hon. Albert D. Shaw, U. S. Consul at Toronto.
Rev. F. K. O'Meara, D.D., Port Hope, Canada.
Rev. A. H. Munro, Toronto.
Rev. J. L. Hurlburt, Plainfield, N. J.
A. O. Van Lennep, Esq., Smyrna, Syria.
Miss Jennie B. Merrill, Normal Training College, New York.
Professor C. H. Scoville, Oran, New York.
Rev. Daniel Marvin, Jun.
Miss Frances E. Willard, Cor. Sec. of Women's National Temperance Union, Chicago.
Miss M. E. Winslow, Secretary of Foreign Sunday School Association, Brooklyn.
J. E. Searles, Jun., Chairman of Executive Committee of International Sunday School Association.
John Fernie, Esq., Sunday School Secretary, of Isle of Wight, England.
R. H. Gilmore, Esq., State Sunday School Secretary for Iowa.

SPECIAL MEETINGS AT THE PARLIAMENT.

THE OPENING EXERCISES.

The International Sunday School Parliament assembled on Tuesday afternoon, July 18th, and spent an hour in short addresses on the social interests of the convention. Rev. Dr. E. O. Haven, President of the Thousand Island Camp Meeting Association, J. E. Searles, of New England, chairman of the "International Sunday School Committee," Mr. and Mrs. Crafts of New Bedford, R. H. Gilmore, of Iowa, and others, participating. A season of hand-shaking and acquaintance-making followed. In the evening a half-hour was spent in a Vesper Service of Scripture and Song, Miss Nellie Brown of Haverhill, Mass., leading the singing. after which the Hon. A. D. Shaw, U. S. Consul at Toronto, was introduced and gave an address, "Christian fraternity and welcome," which was responded to by Rev. A. H. Munro, for Canada; John Fernie, of the Isle of Wight, for Great Britain; Miss M. E. Winslow, of the Foreign Sunday School Association, for the schools of Europe; and A. O. VanLennep for the churches of Asia. J. E. Searles made a short address on the importance of the Sunday School work and of its relation to the future of our country. Rev. Dr. Haven made an interesting and sprightly address as the last of the evening's exercises.

THE SUNDAY SCHOOL OF JULY 23RD.

The first session of the Sunday School of the Thousand Island Parliament was held in the tabernacle on the camp ground at 1.30 A.M., Sunday, July 23rd. The session opened with singing "I Need Thee Every Hour," and a prayer by Superintendent Morton. After reading the Scripture lesson of the day on Responsibility, the school joined in singing the 79th hymn, "What shall the Harvest be." The roll was called as follows :

Pastor—Rev. Richard Newton, D.D., of Philadelphia, Pa.

Superintendent—C. M. Morton, Plymouth Bethel, Brooklyn.

Assistant Superintendents—Jas. Hughes, H. S. Chamberlain.

Chorister—P. P. Bliss.

Secretary—Rev. S. L. Gracey.

Treasurer—Daniel McLean.

Primary Department—Superintendents—Mrs. S. J. Crafts, Miss J. B. Merrill.

Teachers—Revs. B. P. Raymond, A. O. VanLennep, W. S. Hawkes, J. E. Latimer, D.D., F. H. Marling, A. H. Munro, D. J. Marvin, Mrs. W. C. Brewster, Mrs. P. P. Bliss, Revs. Chas. Miles, Wm. Hall, Clark, S. H. Starin, E. C. Curtis, F. Widmer, E. Barras.

A half hour was spent in the study of the lesson of the day, 1 Kings, viii. 5-21, followed by singing, "Oh, think of a home over there."

A review of the lesson was conducted by the pastor, Rev. Dr. Newton, and by Mrs. W. F. Crafts, with the Primary Class. Miss Jennie B. Merrill then explained to the Primary Class a Song, "The Wonderful House," and led them in singing it. Secretary's report was made as follows :—Officers, 7; teachers, 17; scholars, 350; visitors, 72. Total, 446.

Notices were given of the preaching service, and, after a few remarks by the Superintendent, the session was closed with benediction by the pastor.

VAN LENNEP'S ORIENTAL ILLUSTRATIONS OF THE BIBLE.

Rev. Lyman Abbott, D.D., in a letter to *The Christian Union*, says of these instructive entertainments at the Sunday School Parliament :—

Of the *entremets* in the programme we may certainly put first the oriental lectures of A. O. Van Lennep. By birth a Turk, by blood an American, by parentage and personal faith an earnest Christian, by temperament singularly broad-minded, his interpretations of oriental life and character are marvellous, both in interest and instructiveness. He has a wardrobe which ought to make his fortune, if oriental scenes were popular on the stage. He picks up volunteers, whom he trains with rare facility. Every afternoon he gives a new scene from oriental life—to-day, social customs; to-morrow, an Eastern meal, with turbaned and loose-robed guests partaking of it; the next day, the forms of worship, Turkish prayer, Turkish dervishes, the Turkish muezzin calling to prayers. Neither the sermon by Dr. Newton to the children nor the stereopticon pictures attracts or holds a greater or more interested throng than Mr. Van Lennep enacting oriental life and character.

Closing Exercises.

On Wednesday evening, July 26th, the closing exercises of the Sunday School Parliament occurred. Miss Nellie Brown, the talented soprano singer of Grace Church Choir, Haverhill, conducted the music and sang several sacred solos with fine effect. Rev. D. Marvin read a brief address on the "The Past and Possible History of Sunday Schools." Rev. C. H. Payne, D.D., President of Ohio Wesleyan University, followed with an address on "The Rewards of Christian Labor," characterized with the speaker's usual thoughtfulness, earnestness and eloquence.

Rev. W. F. Crafts, the Conductor of all the exercises, said a few farewell words, which were followed by impromptu addresses of thanks and appreciation for his work, from Rev. Lyman Abbott, D.D., Rev. Wm. Hall, Rev. E. Barras and others, and a vote of thanks from the whole congregation. After the formal exercises had closed "Illustrations of the Bible with the Stereopticon" were given by Prof. C. H. Scoville, of Oran, N. Y., whose exhibitions in this line were exceedingly pleasing and profitable, and worthy of wide Christian patronage.

Arrangement of Exercises.

The exercises consisted of addresses, music, and institute sessions on prominent topics of Sunday School work and Bible study. "Methods of Bible Study" and "Bible Readings" were the most prominent subjects. The eight days had each one general topic, and were known as follows :—" Fraternal Day," "Teachers' Day," "Day of Hard Questions," "Childhood Day," "Machinery Day," "Sunday," "Day of Spiritual Work," "Bible Day No. 1," "Bible Day No. 2." Each morning and evening had an "Institute Session," and the afternoon a "Popular Service for Old and Young."

Board and Lodging.

Board and lodgings in tents and cottages on the ground were inexpensive. ($1.50 for both board and lodgings per day.) Ministers and those giving all their time to Christian work, as Y. M. C. A. secretaries, twenty per cent. off. Hotels were also at hand in Alexandra Bay, Clayton, and Gananoque. Steamboats connected with these points before recreation and after the exercises. There were abundant facilities for recreation in croquet, fishing, boating, and steamboat excursions. There was also "music on the river," or "fireworks" nearly every night after the exercises, and many other pleasant diversions.

Rail Roads, &c.

The nearest point to the island on the American side is Clayton, Jefferson Co., N. Y., which may be reached *via* Utica, Rome or Syracuse. On the Canada side, the nearest point is Gananoque, a station on the Grand Trunk R. R., and also of the Royal Mail Steamers, each of which gave half rates for the Parliament. The nearest point by Vermont Central R. R. is Ogdensburg, where steamers connect to Alexandra Bay. This road also gave half rates.

THOUSAND ISLAND PARK AS A SUMMER RESORT.

[*Extracts from the Press.*]

The Committee who have charge of this great gathering are to be congratulated on the scene of the gathering. The matchless beauty of the Thousand Islands camp ground would alone attract many.—*Toronto Evening Telegram.*

No better place could have been selected for such a meeting. The scenery of this glorious river is unsurpassed. Those of your readers who have never seen the St. Lawrence with its islands, its clear, deep green waters, its bold rocky shores, its magnificent rapids, with many noble towns along its banks, should hasten to make the acquaintance.

The attractions for pleasure are fishing, rowing, bathing, sailing, rambling in the woods, making new acquaintances, which is easily done here, watching the boats on the river, etc. This is a place where one may take solid rest, or can have change or breaking up of stagnation, if he desires. If one comes once he will be quite sure to come again.—*S. L. G.*

The Camp Ground on this island is "beautiful for situation" beyond all comparison. If the writer is not mistaken, this place is to have a great growth.—*G. W. H.*

The *Christian Union* in an Editorial on "Summer Camps," suggested by the Sunday School Parliament, says:—

"Apart from their religious aspects, these campings of Christian workers are to be cordially commended for social reasons. The recreations of Americans have been more and more running to luxuries both enervating and expensive. What with summer hops, and carriage bills, and various incidentals, and board at $4.50 a day, the family at Long Branch, Newport or Saratoga have eaten up all the savings of the winter, and the lean kine have been no fatter for their meal. The clamor for expensive luxury in the town or city has not been stayed by expensive luxury in the *pseudo* country. 'Plain country board' is not easy to get; and the problem, What shall we do this summer? is attacked every spring, not with new zeal, but with new anxiety.

"The camp is at once a sign of, and an incentive to, something better. For six weeks you live in an unpainted, unplastered cottage, or beneath canvas. You dispense with kids and silk dresses. You save carriage bills by walking, and substitute a moonlight row on lake or river for a midnight hop. You go to bed as soon after sunset as conversation lags, and rise with the birds. You actually see a sunrise or two. You pay $1.50 or $2 a day instead of $4.50, and make up for the absence of luxuries by the presence of an appetite. Or you keep house on both simpler and cheaper fare; the berries that the children pick and the fish they catch are the staple articles of diet. At the same time, a butcher's tent is not far off, and the hotel will furnish you with a dinner when your own commissariat breaks down. And you are not only surprised to find how little you are really dependent for enjoyment on the luxuries of your ordinary life, but you return to enjoy them with the keener zeal for the temporary abstinence.

"We commend camp life to our readers. We account it a good sign of growing simplicity in taste and life that an increasing number every year are going into camp for their summer relaxation."

RESOLUTIONS.

On July 24th the following resolutions were unanimously adopted:—

The undersigned Sunday School workers, representing various denominations and localities, having enjoyed for several days the privilege of attending the "Sunday School Parliament,' on the Thousand Park, Wellesley Island, in the River St. Lawrence, desire to certify to those who may be invited to similar meetings hereafter:

1. That the Thousand Island region is a delightful summer resort, offering to the seekers of rest and recreation beautiful scenery, pure and cool air, and clear water, at once secluded and accessible.

2. That the location of this camp ground, consisting of 1,000 acres at the south-western extremity of one of the islands, is admirably chosen for the purpose. Its size ensures the amplest provision for all future wants, and protects it against intrusion. The large open, level space on the shore, and the higher, rocky ground further inland, give a pleasant diversity of outline, which have been skilfully made use of in laying out of the avenues and parks. We have seen nothing better suited to the proposed uses.

3. That the public and other buildings erected by the Association are spacious and tasteful, and the management of the trustees is business-like and liberal. We must not withhold our testimony to the excellent quality of the table in the dining hall.

4. We would acknowledge the great pleasure we have had in co-operating with the conductor of the Parliament, Rev. W. F. Crafts, who has proved himself "the right man in the right place," thoroughly informed, versatile and courteous, and of a ready executive gift.

In conclusion, we desire to express the hope that this Parliament may be re-assembled next year.

D. McLean, Toronto; Rev. James W. Stark, Illinois; Chas. M. Morton, Brooklyn; P. P. Bliss, Chicago; A. H. Munro, Toronto; Richard Newton, Philadelphia; James Hughes, Toronto; F. H. Marling, New York; I. S. Connor, Iowa; James E. Latimer, Boston; D. Graham, Montreal.

RECREATION.

Rev. Lyman Abbott, D.D., Editor of the *Christian Weekly*, in an Editorial letter from the "Sunday School Parliament," says :—

"No truer recreation, in the real meaning of that much-abused word can be found, than in a tent or a cottage in some such place as this. The cares of the body are reduced to a minimum. The changing weather is the only leader of fashion; there are no ceremonious visits; the food is sure to be simple, and can be made appetizing. Here there is abundance of superior milk—only four cents a quart—vegetables and fruit in sufficient quantities, all the fresh meat you want, and fish fresh and fine to be had almost for the asking.

"We are in the midst of nature, most beautiful when unadorned. There is a dock where the river steamers land, and where, at any time, you can get a row-boat for a day's fishing or a party can get a steam yacht for an hour's sail. There is a dining-hall where you can get plain and simple fare, but good enough for plain livers, for $1 a day. There are half a dozen cottages scattered through the grounds; in some one of these you can get a room at 50 cents a day. Or you can rent or purchase a lot and put up a tent. And this is evidently the favorite way. These tents are scattered in every direction through the trees.

"Croquet before the door; the hammock by its side; the fishing poles leaning up against a neighboring tree, indicate the favorite occupations.

"Well, I said to my companion as I came away, if I lived in New York, which happily I do not, I should be strongly tempted to buy a couple of lots with two hundred dollars, build the shell of a house with a thousand more, put up a tent or two for the older boys, and come to Thousand Island Park for my summer rest."

CHILDHOOD:
The Text-Book of the Age!

A BOOK FOR PARENTS, TEACHERS, PASTORS, AND ALL LOVERS OF CHILDHOOD.

BY

REV. W. F. CRAFTS,

Author of "Through the Eye to the Heart," "Trophies of Song, "Ideal Sunday School," etc.

12mo. Cloth. Illustrated. Price, $1.50.

In addition to the theoretical portions of the book, parts of which have been received with favor as addresses in New York, Boston, Edinburgh, and other prominent places, and various conventions, there is a

"CHILDHOOD'S DICTIONARY"

Containing 96 striking definitions from the lips of little children. Also a

"CABINET OF SPECIMENS"

Of childhood's characteristic sayings and doings, arranged in scientific order, in "shelves" and "cases," including a choice collection of **350 SPECIMENS.** Parents, teachers (both secular and religious), and all interested in the intellectual or moral development of the young, will find this book a suggestive *introduction to the science of Childhood*, and all lovers of children will secure in the "Cabinet" by far the largest and choicest collection of children's words and deeds that has ever been published. The whole book includes **600 INCIDENTS OF CHILD-LIFE**, which are the scientific data of the theories advanced. They will interest the young as well as adults. The book contains a chapter on the Kindergarten, by Mrs. W. F. Crafts.

OPINIONS OF THE PRESS.

The author has prepared a delightful book on child-nature, life and education; and most clearly shows how little children are the teachers of their superiors in age. The work is charmingly written by one who knows the little folks, and who tells their stories with a fascinating interest for the young and the old. The veriest cynic would warm by its reading. The book will have a large sale, not only from the reputation of the author, but from the rich merits of his pages.—*New England Journal of Education.*

The book will prove a delight to parents and to all interested in young people; and for children themselves from its pages may be extracted a rare fund of amusement. We know of no work which covers quite so much ground in treating of juvenile peculiarities, or accomplishes what is undertaken in its direction more acceptably. The humorous feature of the subject is made prominent throughout. It is beautifully printed upon tinted paper.—*Boston Gazette.*

We hail this book for the very reason that it is a contribution to our understanding of the divine significance of a child. We are glad to notice, also, that Mrs. Crafts has given a chapter on the Kindergarten, which adds to the value of the book.—*Sunday School Times.*

A page of the anecdotes here reproduced, taken regularly three times a day, would cure an obstinate fit of dispepsia.—*Interior (Chicago).*

In each line it is very wise and instructive.—*Christian Intelligencer.*

It is full of bright and witty sayings of the little folks, and is very entertaining.—*Central Christian Advocate.*

We have been very much gratified with the views put forth in this production on the great subject of Christian nurture, the conversion of children, and their early connection with the church. We think them sound and pertinent, and well grounded in experience.—*Christian at Work.*

This work is **an encyclopædia of all that is bright and beautiful in childhood.**—*Buffalo Evening Post.*

It will be a serviceable handbook to all who have to do with the young.—*National Baptist.*

It shows close observation, a deep insight into the child-nature, a care in collating facts referring to the child-life, and a philosophy of child-treatment, nurture, and education, born out of a loving heart. The author, though a clergyman, is a wit, and his volume is well spiced throughout.—*Providence Press.*

It is written in a vivid, stirring style, characteristic of the author, and is a book that we can commend to all ages, but especially to the lovers of children.—*Morning Star.*

Altogether Mr. Crafts' book is one of the best of its kind ever published in this country.—*Hartford Post.*

The author and his wife have contributed to literature, in this volume, something which can hardly be praised too highly, and which must find a place in many households.—*Boston Traveler.*

Sent post-paid, on receipt of price

Lee and Shepard, 41 Franklin Street, Boston, Publishers.

For sale by ADAM MILLER & CO., TORONTO.

RECENT BOOKS BY SPEAKERS AT THE S. S. PARLIAMENT.

For Sale by Adam Miller & Co., Toronto.
Sent by Mail on receipt of price

Sights and Insights, or Knowledge by TRAVEL.
By Rev. H. W. Warren, D.D.
Published by Nelson & Phillips, New York. $1.00.

ILLUSTRATED COMMENTARY ON THE ACTS.
By Rev. Lyman Abbott, D.D.
Published by A. L. Barnes & Co., New York. $1.50.

Through the Eye to the Heart; or, Illustrative TEACHING.
By Rev. W. F. Crafts.
Published by Nelson & Phillips, N. Y. $1.50 (new edition.)

Trophies of Song, or Articles and Incidents in Regard to Sacred Music.
By Rev. W. F. Crafts.
Published by D. Lothrop, Boston. $1.25.

Ideal Sunday School.
By Rev. W. F. Crafts.
Published by Henry Hoyt, Boston. 30 cts.

SERMONS TO CHILDREN.
By Rev. Richard Newton, D.D.
Published by Carter Brothers, N.Y. $1.00 per vol. (12 vols.)

Gospel Songs for Sunday Schools and Prayer Meetings.

BY P. P. BLISS.

Published by JOHN CHURCH & CO., CINCINNATTI.

35 Cents each.

Open Letters to Primary Teachers,

WITH

Helpful Hints for Intermediate Teachers.

BY MRS. W. F. CRAFTS.

Published by NELSON & PHILIPS, NEW YORK.

Price, $1.00

SONGS FOR LITTLE FOLKS

IN THE HOME AND SCHOOL.

BY

MRS. W. F. CRAFTS AND MISS JENNY B. MERRILL.

Published by BIGELOW & MAIN, NEW YORK.

30 cents in boards.

THE LESSON COMPEND.,

A COLLECTION OF THE BEST THINGS IN THE COMMENTARIES ON THE INTERNATIONAL LESSONS OF EACH YEAR.

BY

REV. J. L. HURLBUT.

Published each year by NELSON & PHILLIPS, N. Y.

Price, 50 cents.

www.ingramcontent.com/pod-product-compliance
Lightning Source LLC
Chambersburg PA
CBHW020244170426
43202CB00008B/223